DONKEY BRIDGES FOR DEVELOPMENTAL TA

MAKING TRANSACTIONAL ANALYSIS ACCESSIBLE
AND MEMORABLE

Julie Hay has been active within the transactional analysis community for many years. She is a past president of both the European and the International Transactional Analysis Associations - EATA and ITAA. She served as Vice Chair of the UK-based Institute of Transactional Analysis and was one of the three founders and then inaugural chairperson of the UK-based Institute of Developmental Transactional Analysis.

In 2009 she founded the International Centre for Developmental Transactional Analysis - www.icdta.net.

She has also set up the International Centre for Developmental Super-Vision - www.icdsv.net.

Julie has designed several TA qualifications that she provides in cooperation with an international group of TA colleagues, all of whom have accreditation from the International and/or European Associations. See www.icdta.net and www.icdsv.net for details or contact Julie on julie@adinternational.com.

Julie continues to provide ongoing TA training within the UK and currently leads programmes in the Ukraine, Poland and Turkey - www.adinternational.com. She regularly works in other countries and is available as a pro bono 'travelling trainer' under the auspices of ITAA and EATA for groups in economically-disadvantaged areas of the world.

Julie provides consultancy services, coaching and supervision by arrangement. In addition to transactional analysis, Julie has many years experience of designing and running assessment and development centres, and of setting up in-house mentoring and coaching schemes. She is also a Licensed NLP (neuro linguistic programming) Trainer.

She was a founder and then President 2006-2008 of the European Mentoring and Coaching Council.

The questionnaires contained in this book can be purchased from www.sherwoodpublishing.com

Related books by the same author

Transactional Analysis for Trainers 2nd edition, Sherwood 2009
The 1st edition of this book appeared in French as *Analyse Transactionnelle et Formation,* Desclée de Brouwer 1994
The 2nd edition appears in Polish as *Analiza Transakcyjna dla trenerów Kraków* : Grupa Doradczo-Szkoleniowa Transmisja 2010

Working it Out at Work - Understanding Attitudes and Building Relationships 2nd edition Sherwood 2009
The 1st edition of this book is translated into:
Slovenian as *Uspesni na delu*, Potr itev d.n.o. 1999
Romanian as *Sarada de la serviciu*, CODECS 2006
Dutch as *We lossen het samen wel op – Transactionele Analyse op de werkvloer*, SWP Publishers 2004
Persian as *Success Psychology in the Workplace*, Roshd, 1991

Dealing with Difficult People - Workbook and Tape Set, Sherwood 1998

Transactional Analysis Introductory Course – Workbook & Tape Set, Sherwood 2001

Neuro-Linguistic Programming Practitioner Course – Workbook and Tape Set, Sherwood 2001

Reflective Practice and Supervision for Coaches, Open University Press 2007

Transformational Mentoring: Creating Developmental Alliances for Changing Organizational Cultures, McGraw-Hill 1995, Sherwood 1999

Action Mentoring, Sherwood 1997

DONKEY BRIDGES FOR DEVELOPMENTAL TA

MAKING TRANSACTIONAL ANALYSIS ACCESSIBLE AND MEMORABLE

Julie Hay

SHERWOOD PUBLISHING
∙ ∙ ● developing people

HERTFORD UK

Published by

Sherwood Publishing

Wildhill, Broadoak End, Hertford SG14 2JA, UK

www.sherwoodpublishing.com

email: sherwood@adinternational.com

This edition first published 2012

A catalogue record of this book is available from the British Library.

ISBN 978-1-907037-02-3

Design by Diane Richardson info@drdm.eu

Drawings by Peter Emery

Printed by Lightning Source, www.lightningsource.com 2012

TO DAN, BEN, JOSH, GABE AND NOAH

the next generation to bring me such joy
and prove that 'scripty' behaviour
can lead to wonderful consequences

CONTENTS

LIST OF FIGURES

ACKNOWLEDGEMENTS

My thanks to the originators of the theories - without them there would have been no topics to convert into donkey bridges.

My thanks to the many people who have taught TA to me - especially those of you who have provided the basis for the ways I teach it.

My thanks to the people who have attended the workshops I've run - and helped me to create even better donkey bridges.

ABOUT THIS BOOK

The first edition of this book emerged from my preparation for a session I was to run at an international TA conference in Aruba in 1994. I was asked to provide my 'speech' to the Japanese interpreter so I started writing. In the end, I had far too much material for a conference session, all of the Japanese attendees knew English well enough not to need an interpreter, and I had the content for a book which has sold steadily ever since.

I want to emphasise that the conference session and this book were designed for those who already have a reasonable knowledge of TA and want to apply it to help other people to develop themselves. I have therefore kept explanations of the TA concepts to a minimum and provided you with references to sources of additional information. These sources include the originators of the ideas which I have taken and turned into donkey bridges.

Teaching TA from this book alone is not good practice. The book is intended to give you ideas for presenting TA in ways that are easy to understand and memorable. The book does not give you the background detail that you need to develop a professional level of knowledge and competence. It is not a substitute for serious TA study – to use the ideas as they stand would be like learning some vocabulary and then attempting to speak a language without any knowledge of the syntax.

I was first introduced to TA in the 1970's. I rapidly began to question the focus on pathology. I recall suggesting that we would get on better with people if we matched their drivers but was told that this was a bad idea. Later, I developed the notion of working styles as the positive side of drivers – and I have continued to devise positive ways of applying the range of TA concepts. It seems to me that we construct our own meanings based on our context. Developmental TA is about growth so we need positive models that move us on; psychotherapy is about cure so needs models that allow understanding of the deeper pathological processes. Nowadays, I realise that developmental TA fits the positive psychology approach (Seligman 2002). And therefore so do these donkey bridges.

STRUCTURE OF THE BOOK

I have structured the book into sections to make it easier for you to find donkey bridges for specific topics. I start by explaining the terms 'developmental TA' and 'donkey bridges', both in ways that you might use to describe TA and how you teach it to your own clients, participants or students.

Then I go on to review contracting and several related elements that fit with presenting TA to others in a professional manner.

Next are donkey bridges related to the key aim of TA – autonomy – and how scripts can be presented to create a more flexible and positive perception. After that I've presented windows on the world because this links so much with script to create our frames of reference.

I continue with a section on AP^3: the Assessing Cube to pull together donkey bridges relating to various models of ego states including personal styles, working styles, leadership styles and stroking preferences and processes.

Then a section on what goes on inside, how that shows up as behaviour, what then happens in groups, followed by some ways of analysing organisations rather than individuals.

The final sections cover leadership, how to manage change, and finally how to develop your own competence as a practitioner.

COPYRIGHT

SECTION 1: DEVELOPMENTAL TA

THE OLD PERSON AND THE FLOOD STORY

There once was an old person who lived in the same house that they had been born in. The old person had lived there for many years.

One day, it started to rain. It rained. And it rained. And it rained. And the land around started to flood.

After a while, a farmer came along on a tractor. The old person could hear the noise of the tractor coming closer. When it was near the house, the farmer called to the old person "I've come to save you from the flood".

But the old person said "I've lived here all my life. This is my home. My God will take care of me. I'm staying here."

So the neighbour went away in the tractor. The sound of the tractor faded into the distance. And it rained. And it rained. And it rained. And the flood grew deeper.

And after a while, a police officer came along in a police rescue launch. The old person could hear the noise of the police sirens coming closer. When the launch was near the house, the police officer called out to the old person "I've come to save you from the flood. Come with me."

But the old person said "I've lived here all my life. This is my home. My God will take care of me. I'm staying here."

So the police officer went away in the police launch. The sound of the police sirens faded into the distance. And it rained. And it rained. And it rained. And the flood grew deeper.

After a while, a pilot came along in a helicopter. The old person could hear the noise of the helicopter rotors as it came closer. When it was near the house, the pilot called to the

old person "I've come to save you from the flood. Come with me."

But the old person said "I've lived here all my life. This is my home. My God will take care of me. I'm staying here."

So the pilot went away in the helicopter. The sound of the helicopter rotors faded into the distance. And it rained. And it rained. And it rained. And the flood grew deeper. And the old person drowned!

And so the old person met their God. And the old person complained to their God "Why did you let me drown? Why didn't you help me?"

And their God said "Who do you think sent you the tractor, the police launch and the helicopter?"

THEORY, TECHNIQUES AND TOOLS

This story you've just read illustrates the essence of transactional analysis. Eric Berne wrote about each of us having an Adult ego state that could process the here-and-now. He taught TA to patients so they could work out how to change themselves. We need to:

- teach the clients the **theory**,
- help them learn how to apply the **techniques**,
- and make sure that they realise that they must use the **tools** themselves

A key principle of developmental TA can be stated as:

we are not broken: **we are growing**

we don't need fixing: **we need fertiliser**

THE PRACTITIONER'S PICKAXE

Sometimes it seems as if we are like seeds that have been cast on the ground and covered with concrete. If someone with a pickaxe comes along and cracks the concrete, we will emerge and grow towards the light. We will do that even better if they give us a supply of nourishment - and better still if they arrange protection from the elements until we are strong enough to cope on our own.

As practitioners, we carry the pickaxe and know how to make the cracks.

DTA, then, is TA as applied by the non-therapy fields. It fits the classical school of TA in style although it borrows theories from across the range of TA approaches.

The message about self-help is particularly relevant for developmental TA. In psychotherapy and therapeutic counselling applications of TA, the therapist/counsellor and client usually agree to work together over a period of time. For organisational, educational and counselling/coaching applications we often have only a limited time with people. Perhaps they have come on a training course and we will not see them again after that. Maybe we have gone into their organisation as a facilitator or coach and will only be there until a specific project is completed.

We must also take into account that there are generally more than two parties to the contract. In addition to practitioner and 'client', there may be an organisation in the form of a senior manager, human resources professional or head teacher, perhaps also the line manager of our client(s), or the pupils and their parents in a school setting. Any of these stakeholders may be able to cancel the contract at any time.

We need methods, therefore, that can be taught quickly, that are easy to understand, and can be used when we are no longer around – hence the donkey bridges.

SECTION 2:   DONKEY BRIDGES

So what are donkey bridges? The term comes from Germany where trainers use Eselsbrücken to mean those ways in which we help people learn and recall.

Donkeys are hard working, friendly animals who feel good when you stroke them. They need to be helped over bridges. This is because their frame of reference is limited so they have trouble imagining how pleasant it will be to go into new territory. Once we help them across the bridge they can enjoy themselves in new fields. The more bridges we help them over, the more adventurous they become.

There are seven types of donkey bridges I use and I have invented a donkey bridge to recall them, which is: "*Someone approached and gave plenty of lovely workable ideas!*"

The donkey bridge types are: *stories, alliteration, gimmicks, pictures, labels, words, involvement.*

The rest of this booklet consists of a series of examples of donkey bridges. Some will utilise one element only; others will be a combination of story, picture, involvement, gimmick, alliteration and/or label.

STORIES
Stories help us recall because they provide a structure. If you give one group a list of items to memorise in a very short time (such as just long enough to read the list of bull, rod,

cycle, sunshine, morning, fish, walk, pain, field, river, picnic) and give another group the same list but in an order that allows them to quickly discern the potential story (when listed as morning, cycle, rod, river, fish, sunshine, picnic, walk, field, bull, pain), the second group will recall more words and more accurately (the others often add words that are not there!)

Stories as donkey bridges include fairy stories, jokes, examples drawn from real life - anything in which there are characters and something happens. Eric Berne wrote lots of short stories entitled Cyprian St. Cyr, in which he often used the same characters. Each little vignette had a moral or a challenging question to consider. In the same way, personal anecdotes, self disclosures by the trainer, and case studies all help to make the training content more vivid.

The story you read earlier about *The Old Person and the Flood* demonstrates how we can use a story as a metaphor. The underlying message in this story is that knowledge of TA is not enough - we must be prepared to use what we are offered. This is a powerful story to use during a training course, especially when participants raise doubts about whether "it" (meaning TA) will "work" (meaning make a difference). The fact that the story is also a joke increases the impact.

Similar stories from the early years of TA are the Warm Fuzzy Tale (Steiner 1969) (see the section later on Strokes for an updated version of this) and Berne's story about the monkey (see later under Autonomy and Script). The use of fairy story labels for scripts (Little Red Riding, Cinderella etc.) and of myths for process scripts (Tantalus, Arachne, etc.) are also donkey bridges. Provided we already know the fairy stories or myths, we find it easier to understand and remember TA concepts.

Metaphors often contain more than we intend, or are consciously aware of. It is, therefore, a sensible precaution to check before you use one for EEEE:
- **embody** - what do you or others feel when you think of or tell this story, what impact does it have kinaesthetically?
- **encompass** - how widely does this story extend into your own or a client's existence; what areas of life does it encompass?
- **empower** - what 'power' does the story provide; how could you adjust the story to make it (even) more empowering?
- **entail** - what are some of the 'hidden' consequences of living as if this story were true?

For example, a team of top managers in India decided that their organisation was like an elephant – slow to start moving but once it did move, no-one could stop it. What they nearly overlooked was that it had no idea of what was going on around the back of it, where the smaller, more manoeuvrable competitors were gaining customers by being so much more flexible and quick to meet the customers' changing requirements.

ALLITERATION

Some people hate alliteration so when I use it I point out that they are free to change to words that start with different letters. Misery is optional!

So far I have used alliteration twice, for *theory - techniques – tools* and *embody - encompass - empower - entail.*

Later in this book I will suggest more, such as *awareness + alternatives + authenticity + attachment = autonomy*, and that we need objectives that are *measurable, manageable and motivational.*

Other examples will include several that relate also to pictures, gimmicks and labels. We can often merge several types of donkey bridge for greater impact. Thus, the picture of the Sailship Success will have sails all beginning with "s", as will the Steps to Success. Our stroke preferences linked to drivers can all start with "p" and our characteristics with "c". Life positions have an "h", or an "a" if we relate them to assertiveness.

Alliteration will not necessarily translate so new sets of words will be needed for other languages. I invite you to be creative.

GIMMICKS

Gimmicks are devices for attracting attention, which is why Berne wrote that games begin with gimmicks and cons. We can use small strips of differently coloured Velcro as a gimmick to teach people about games. If several people are given one side of Velcro only, and told to move around and see what happens when they touch 'their' Velcro to someone else's, they will find that they "connect" with some people and not with others. This demonstrates how we play games only when we meet someone with a corresponding set of hooks. It also shows that we have to have had our own set of hooks in the first place. If we had no hooks of our own, they could not hook us into a game!

Gimmicks, then, when teaching developmental TA, are any devices we use to get the point across. Making up little books and small sticky squares of paper to illustrate trading stamps is another example. Taking along a can of talcum powder (or borrowing a salt cellar from the dining room of a Training Centre) will reinforce the point that people need to use the TA they learn; change will not just miraculously happen to them. We can shake out some talc or salt to demonstrate our lack of magical powers to make other people change, whilst pointing out that

shake and make is a fake

Referring to the silver lining of good intentions, the platinum rule for treating others as they prefer, and the golden bridge for creating a relationship, are also gimmicks.

Under alliteration, I mentioned measurable, manageable, motivational for objective settings – a gimmick for this is to link it to M&M's sweets as described later in the Change section.

PICTURES

Pictures make excellent donkey bridges because we remember far more if we see it as well as hear it. This is why it is so important that trainers use visual aids - which should be CRISP:

- **clear** - large print size, can be seen from the back of the room.
- **reinforcing** - covers the important points, matches the verbal content
- **interesting** - uses colours, pictures, cartoons, variety
- **simple** - key points only, outline diagrams, easy to absorb
- **presented** - shown for long enough, removed when dealt with, not obscured by presenter

CRISP visual aids

- Clear
- Reinforcing
- Interesting
- Simple
- Presented

We can paint verbal pictures by describing scenes in detail. We can also be our own pictures, such as when we demonstrate behavioural elements of ego states by folding our arms parentally, or fidgeting like a child.

Diagrams are also pictures and are particularly significant within TA. The script matrix and autonomy matrix shown later are effective donkey bridges provided people are familiar with the three stacked circles diagram for a person's ego states.

In later sections there are some more pictures I use, including the Sailship Success to highlight key elements of organisations, a set of Steps to Success to represent the six treatment levels on the discount matrix, and Windows on the World as life positions.

When using pictures or diagrams, as with metaphors, beware of embedded but unintended messages. The script matrix as shown in many TA books follows Berne, who drew the arrows from parents to child so that they 'cut into' the ego states of the little person. This gives a strong yet unconscious message that something was inserted into you that may be hard to remove (and may be much more painful than a tonsillectomy).

Compare also the script matrix with the autonomy matrix – and recognise the different impact between a picture that has parents apparently pushing the child down versus one where they appear to be holding the child up.

LABELS

Berne used lots of labels that were catchy, intriguing, simple and often related to everyday words. Parent, Adult, Child, for instance. Script, strokes, gallows laughs, rackets, trading stamps, games, electrode, Little Professor. Fanita English provided hot potato, which conjures up a very appropriate image, and Sleepy, Spunky and Spooky for the parts of the Child ego state.

Some existing TA labels have become so well used that many people outside the TA community no longer know the source. Examples include strokes and games people play. You will see later that I have also changed the names for some games because the original names were politically incorrect and likely to cause offence.

I convert other TA labels to make them more suitable for developmental applications. Life positions become windows on the world; ego states are personal styles (for behaviour) and thinking styles (for what goes on inside us); drivers are our working styles.

Some TA labels I retain because they are unusual and therefore cause people to stop and think. These include: group imagoes - images means almost the same but sounds far too ordinary; discounting - where the explanation of how we deduct a percentage of ourselves, people and situations emphasises how peculiar we can be; rackets - because we can then tell a story about protection rackets, where gangsters manipulate people by cleverly veiled threats of what will happen if they don't behave.

WORDS

I borrow from NLP to demonstrate the potentially hypnotic effect of the words we use. My colleague Peter Emery and I devised a way of classifying the various language patterns and using a hand as a memory aid, as shown in Figure 2.1.

Missing Information

- *Deletion* is when we leave something out of the surface structure e.g. I am confused (but we don't say what about).
- *Comparisons* are when we use comparators to indicate differences without providing full information. e.g. It is better to do it this way.
- *Unspecified Referential Index* occurs when we don't give details of who did something. e.g. They don't listen.
- *Unspecified Verbs* are those process words which are not explicit enough to make the action clear. e.g. Do it now.
- *Nominalisations* are abstract nouns that arise when we turn a process into an event. Loving becomes love, trusting becomes trust. A simple test for a nominalisation is to check whether it would fit into a wheelbarrow! If it won't, it's an abstract. e.g. I broke off the relationship.

Figure 2.1: Language Pattern Formats

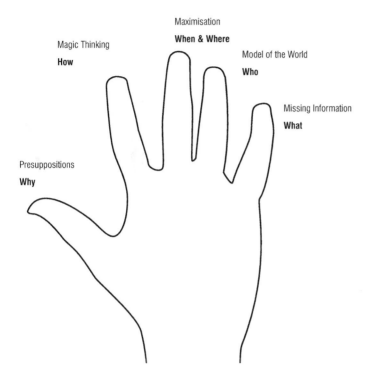

Model of the World
- *Modal* Operators are the words that represent rules and boundaries to which we unconsciously adhere. e.g. We must do it this way - or - I can't do it.
- *Lost Performatives* are generalisations about the world which the speaker has based on their own experiences. e.g. This is how we should do it.

Maximisation
- *Universal quantifiers* are generalisations. (In TA jargon, grandiosity) They may incorporate words such as all, always, never, none. e.g. It always happens.
- *General Referential Index* occurs when we generalise an attribute of one thing or one person onto a group of them e.g. All dogs are vicious. The 'rule' may also be implied within the sentence pattern e.g. Dogs are vicious.

Magic Thinking
- *Cause - Effect* are distortions where the sentence structure links two (or more) different concepts as if one causes the other. e.g. You make me angry.
- *Complex Equivalence* is when two statements are linked so that they appear to be equivalent and mean the same thing. e.g. You don't kiss me any more – you don't love me.

- *Mind reading* is often an intuitive response to non-verbal clues. However, it may also be hallucination and/or projection of our feelings onto others. e.g. You don't love me anymore.

Presuppositions

- *Presuppositions* are the assumptions that are built into the words we use. They are things that must be true for the sentence to have meaning. e.g. When did you stop picking your nose?

If we want to help learners, we need to pay careful attention to our use of words and avoid language that unwittingly places limitations.

INVOLVEMENT

It may seem superfluous to include involvement as a donkey bridge. Obviously, if people are involved enough to be applying TA models to themselves, they are likely to remember it. However, we can use a variety of activities to reinforce learning points. For example, I use the game described below of Elephants and Giraffes to illustrate working styles. There are similar childlike activities that will generate just enough stress in grown-ups that they can sense their drivers turning on.

Elephants and Giraffes – how to play

Before playing this, check and arrange alternative movements for anyone with a physical impairment that would affect how they join in.

Group forms a circle and someone stands in the centre - usually the facilitator at first to give a demonstration.

The person in the centre shuts their eyes, spins round, stops, opens eyes and points immediately to someone whilst calling out "Elephant" or "Giraffe".

If "Elephant" is called, the person pointed at should raise an arm in front of them with their hand hanging down to resemble a trunk. The people on either side bend their arms to form the shape of an ear on each side of the trunk of the 'elephant'.

If "Giraffe" is called, the person pointed at raises an arm above their head to resemble the animal's long neck. The people on either side bend down so their arm nearest the 'giraffe' is pointing to the floor to create an extra leg for the animal – 4 legs in all.

Whoever moves slowest or gets it wrong changes places with the person in the middle.

They then shut their eyes, spin, open eyes and point whilst calling out "Elephant" or "Giraffe" – and so on.

The game runs until you judge that it has lasted long enough to illustrate drivers (or working styles) and you can review what happened: Hurry ups focus on playing quickly; Be Perfects pay attention to arms being moved to the 'correct' position; Please People worry about spoiling the fun for others; Be Strongs hate the whole silly process; and Try Hards may suddenly add different animals ("Penguin" – 2 arms flapping in front like flippers with arms of people on either side also as penguin feet!).

We can use involvement in other ways too. The activity mentioned earlier about using strips of Velcro to illustrate game dynamics is an example - and making the group wait for the explanation is also a way of keeping them involved!

When the story of The Old Person and the Flood is told, it can be with audience participation, with the listeners   providing the sound effects - of the rain, the flood, the tractor, the siren on the launch, and the helicopter.

Contracting is a technique that cannot be used without Involvement. Telling the audience what you propose to offer is not contracting; they must at least signify that this matches their expectations. It is usually much better, of course, to go into more detail about their requirements, as you will see in the next section.

SECTION 3:   CONTRACTING

To ensure we operate professionally to meet the client's needs and not what we think they should want, we need to contract. Contracting is a basic principle in TA - if no contract has been established we are not truly applying TA.

Contracts may or may not be written down. A verbal contract is still a contract. The main point is that we discuss and agree why we are interacting when we plan to use TA to help someone grow.

No contract = No TA

P6 LEVELS
Contracts operate at different levels - all levels need to be clear to avoid unwitting sabotage.
- **Procedural** - administrative details, such as when shall we meet, where, how often, who keeps notes, what are the payment routines, cancellation procedures?
- **Professional** - what am I offering as professional analyst, trainer, consultant, educator, mentor, coach, etc., what does the client need, how competent am I to meet those needs, how much is being paid for my services, what is the client prepared to do to contribute to their own development?
- **Purpose** - why are we coming together, what do you, and any other parties to the contract, and the client, want to achieve, how will you (both/all) know when it has been attained?
- **Personal** - how will we relate to each other, how friendly or remote will we be, what is an appropriate interaction style e.g. nurturing, challenging, problem-solving?
- **Psychological** - what might occur outside our awareness, how might either (or any) of us sabotage the process?
- **Physis** - how does the purpose fit with the client's overall growth and development, is it ecologically sound for them, how does the work fit with my own urge to develop my potential as helping professional?

THE EYES IN THE CORNERS
A key point of Fanita English's (1975) article on the three cornered contract was that people fantasise about what the other parties have agreed between them. To demonstrate this, I draw eyeballs in each corner to emphasise that each stakeholder should have knowledge of the contracts between others (this need not include the content of what then gets talked about).

Figure 3.1: The Eyes in the Corners

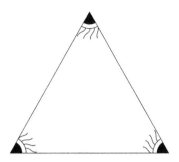

PROTECTION, PERMISSION AND POTENCY

We can link the P6 contract levels to:

- **Protection** – *procedural* – clarity rather than misunderstandings, structure and boundaries to 'protect' the client
  – *professional* – only what I am competent to offer, so the client gets the most skilled interventions possible
- **Permission** – *purpose* – indicating to the client, directly and indirectly, that they can achieve
  – *personal* – agreeing how to interact, in ways that are allowing and enabling
- **Potency** – *psychological* – underlying dynamics are brought to the surface, talking about the elephant (or the fish) under the table
  - *physis* – the client's natural urge to grow will provide the impetus

Figure 3.2: P3+6

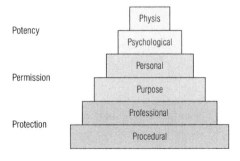

Anne de Graaf suggests another way to define Crossman's (1966) three P's (reproduced here with Anne's permission):

Potency = Priest, who makes connection with a greater power

Permission = Prophet, who helps client see possibilities

Protection = Pastor, who takes care of the well-being of the client

ETHICAL MANIPULATION

When taught ways of interacting more skilfully with others, people often worry that they are simply learning to manipulate. This is true! Everything we do manipulates in some way. We look at someone and they have a reaction. We speak and they must decide whether to reply. Manipulation is often associated with deceit or trickery - however it also means dealing skilfully (as when artists manipulate materials, especially with their hands).

The principles of ethical manipulation are:

- **recognise** - be aware of our own motives, of the preferences and needs of others
- **respect** - the rights of other people to have different expectations and desires
- **respond** - in ways that take account of other people's styles

R4C4P4 GROUNDRULES

The following is a checklist for inviting participants to establish groundrules for working together. You can invite a group to consider which of the following might be relevant to them.

Respect - all opinions are respected and valued, all have equal rights, all will be treated respectfully, we will assume positive intentions.

Responsibility - groundrules can only exist if all involved agree and take personal responsibility. Each person needs to indicate clearly to the rest of the group, including the facilitator, whether they accept shared responsibility for the groundrules – and for asking for re-negotiation if necessary.

Relationship – much development comes from being supported by others, so the group needs to consider how they will support each other, how they will establish close and trusting relationships.

Results – need to remember purpose, such as to bring about change in the organisation, better management, etc – groundrules need to reflect this emphasis on achieving results and not being simply somewhere to 'talk about' problems.

Confidentiality - no-one gossips – what is said in the group room stays in the room (unless the person(s) who said it agrees otherwise).

Commitment – to the group and to ourselves – what we say we will do, we do – or we will explain why we changed our mind.

Communication – active listening, one person speaks at a time, plenty of paraphrasing and summarising to minimise misunderstandings.

Challenge – valuable learning comes from feedback – need to give each other honest, constructive criticism (balance challenge and support).

Participation - everyone participates – there will be a range of activities designed to foster learning – in addition to our own learning, we can help others learn by joining in, giving feedback.

Privacy - everyone has the right to pass – to decide not to reveal personal information about themselves, not to give specific feedback to another person.

Preparation– all will come prepared to each session, having done any assignments, updated action plans, etc.

Practicalities – in the real world, things happen that make us late. Time, on the other hand, does not wait. Need to agree how long group will wait for latecomers or whether to start exactly on time anyway – what is the routine for people to advise the group or the facilitator if they will be late or missing. (hotel tel no, facilitator's mobile, how long beforehand, etc); what to do about updating people who miss a session.

SECTION 4: AUTONOMY AND SCRIPT

AUTONOMY

Autonomy is the aim of teaching people TA. To be autonomous we need:

- **awareness** - being in the here-and-now, knowing who we and others really are
- **alternatives** - having several options for how we might behave, being able to choose what to do
- **authenticity** - knowing that we can be our real selves and still be OK, not having to wear a mask
- **attachment** - being able to connect and bond with other people

Three Keys to Autonomy

A valuable set of reminders that helps us maintain autonomy as we interact with people is:

- look for the **silver lining** in others, assume they have good intentions and stay curious to find out what these are even when they are behaving negatively.
- remember the **platinum rule** - do unto others as they would be done by (not as you would be done by).
- offer them a **golden bridge** - an easy way to come towards you and create a relationship, or a face-saving route if they need to change their minds or behave differently.

These three valuable keys to autonomy - the silver lining, the platinum rule and the golden bridge - are all easier to achieve if we do as the American Indians suggest - walk in the other person's moccasins for at least a mile. If we put ourselves in their shoes and do our best to share their frame of reference, we will be better able to connect with them.

Maybe

The following story illustrates the advantages, and a style, of being in the here-and-now!

There was once a farmer who had a very nice horse that was admired by all the villagers. However, one day the horse jumped the fence and galloped away. The villagers all said to the farmer what bad luck that was for him – and the farmer just looked at them and said "Maybe."

A few days later the horse came back, bringing with it a number of wild horses that the farmer could make his own. The villagers said what good luck that was for him and the farmer just looked at them and said "Maybe."

The following week the farmer's son was riding one of the wild horses, attempting to train it, when the horse threw him and he broke his leg. The villagers all said to the farmer what bad luck that was for him – and the farmer just looked at them and said "Maybe."

A few days later the Army came to the village, taking the young men away as conscripts to fight in a war. They didn't take the farmer's son because he had a broken leg. The villagers said what good luck that was for him and the farmer just looked at them and said "Maybe."

SHOULDN'TS

Chris Davidson developed a donkey bridge to help us recall the 12 injunctions identified by Bob and Mary Goulding (1976) (included here with permission from Chris):

- Self – Don't be you (sex you are)
- Health – Don't be well/Don't be sane
- Others – Don't belong/Don't be close/Don't trust/Don't love
- Understanding – Don't think, don't think X
- Life – Don't be/Don't exist
- Development – Don't grow up/Don't be a child
- Needs – Don't be important
- Tasks – Don't (do anything), Don't make it (succeed)
- Sensation – Don't feel, don't feel Y

SHOULDSS

We can convert SHOULDN'TS to SHOULDSS to cover the permissions (needing an extra S on the end):

- Self – be who you are
- Health – be psychologically healthy
- Others – be emotionally and physically close to others
- Understanding – think
- Life – live
- Development – be your age
- Sensation – be aware of sensations and emotions
- Succeed – succeed in whatever way is healthy for you

SCRIPT

Most writing about scripts in the TA literature has focused on the negative elements. Fanita English writes of the positive uses of script – we need some structure in our lives.

We can thus separate scripts into **developmental** or **deterministic**.

Script Matrix

As a picture, the script matrix will have more impact at the unconscious level than we may realise. As I mentioned when describing picture donkey bridges, Berne drew solid lines from the parents into the ego states of the child - the implication was that the parents inserted messages and the child was powerless.

It gives a much more hopeful message if we use a matrix where there are dotted lines from the caregivers. It is even more hopeful if these lines don't reach the child. This conveys the meaning that our script messages are our interpretations and were generally picked up at the ulterior, or psychological, level. Whatever the caregiver did or said, they did not insert the messages into us - we interpreted and we decided.

Figure 4.1: Script Matrix

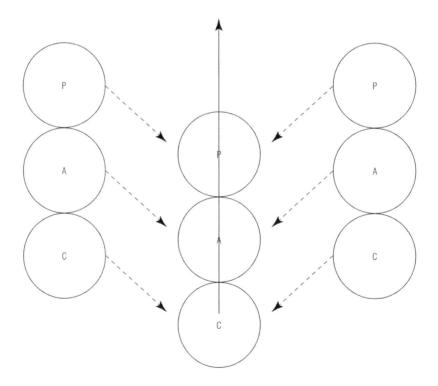

We made up our own minds about the script messages. We can therefore change our minds. This is the decisional nature of TA. Physis is our own natural urge to grow and develop and to do so we can change old decisions and make new ones.

To emphasise this principle of human growth, it is a good idea to include the aspiration arrow whenever we draw the script matrix. It is also important that we show it extending above the height of the caregivers, to signal that we can grow beyond any limitations they may have had.

The reason we fail to make new decisions sometimes is that we are in trance-ference (transference) and countertrance-ference (countertransference). We have hypnotised ourselves when we were young and now we continue to put ourselves into trance so that we regress and repeat old patterns. In trance-ference we hallucinate that we and other people in the present are really in the past. In counter-transference they do the same to us. I have included more about transference later.

The Autonomy Matrix

Drawing the matrix, as shown in Figure 4.2, with the parents/caregivers below the child gives a very different impression – now they are holding the child up supportively rather

Figure 4.2: Autonomy Matrix

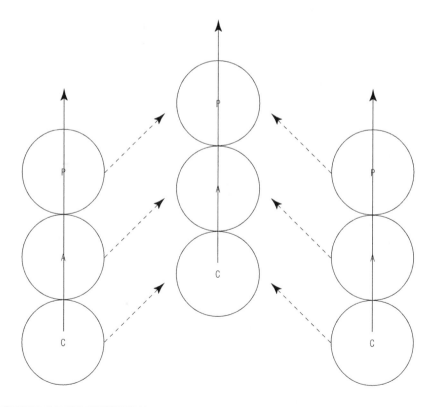

than pushing the child down. Also, Trudi Newton pointed out to me that we can add the aspiration arrows for the caregivers as well.

The Monkey, the Parrot and the Bubble

Whenever we apply developmental TA, our hope is that people will become more autonomous. There are two stories in the early TA literature that are particularly relevant. They convey similar messages - that we can change more quickly and more easily than we imagine.

Eric Berne's (1968) version refers to a monkey.

There is a young boy (or girl, or child) whose parents tie a monkey onto his chest when he is very small. They do this to be helpful - indeed most of their friends do the same thing for their children. It restricts the boy's movement so there are some things he cannot do. However, he trusts his parents so he learns to work around the restrictions or to fit in with them. And the monkey keeps him safe and stops him doing things that his parents believe are dangerous.

However, when he grows up he begins to notice that some people seem to have no monkey. They can do whatever they like. So he thinks he will see about getting the monkey removed.

He goes to a doctor, who looks carefully at the knots in the string holding the monkey in place. The doctor then says that the knots are very complicated and will take many months to unravel, and quotes an hourly fee for the sessions. The man decides that sounds too expensive and decides not to bother.

Time goes by and the man gets more and more uncomfortable about the restrictions imposed by having the monkey. So he goes to another doctor.

This doctor examines the knots very thoroughly. The doctor then says that the knots are very complicated, and have been there a long time. They may even take years to unravel, and quotes an even higher hourly rate for sessions. Again, the man decides not to bother, although this time he feels disappointed.

More time goes by. Eventually, the man goes to yet another doctor. This one takes out a large pair of scissors and cuts the string. The monkey bounds free.

Brian Allen (1971) provides a similar story, except that instead of a monkey there is a parrot.

Suzy (or Shipra, or Sophie) was a small girl who had an older brother Simon (or Servaas, or Suliman). Suzy's parents were busy so they told Simon to take care of her. Simon was still quite young himself so this was a big responsibility. So he listened carefully to what their parents said to Suzy about how she should behave. He then taught the parrot to say the same things, such as "Don't answer back", "Look after other people" and "Be a good girl".

Simon then put the parrot onto Suzy's head. Now he could play and read and do whatever he wanted to do without having to pay attention to Suzy all the time. The parrot did it for him.

When Suzy grew up, she still had the parrot on her head telling her what to do and what not to do. This interfered quite a lot with her life. The parrot often objected to her making friends or being confident or enjoying herself. Suzy often felt miserable when she followed the parrot's instructions.

One day, Suzy went to a doctor and asked for help. The doctor told her it would take many years to cure her and gave her some pills. Suzy felt even more depressed.

Eventually, Suzy went to another doctor for help. This time, the doctor said all Suzy needed to do was get rid of the parrot. Suzy was doubtful about this because she was used to having the parrot there. She thought also that the parrots claws were tangled into her hair and it would be painful to pull them out.

However, this doctor smiled and said Suzy just needed a little help. Then the doctor reached out, grabbed the parrot and threw it out the window. It squawked once and flew away for ever.

Berne's story has a kinaesthetic base - the monkey metaphor invites the listener to connect the story to the way they feel. Allen's story relates directly to our auditory channels, as we recognise the voices in our heads that we replay from the past. A visual version might be to have the grown-ups keep the child in a special protective bubble. This bubble is intended to ensure that the child does not have to face unpleasant facts of life. Although done originally to keep the child safe, the bubble means that vision is interfered with. Sometimes the bubble will make things look nicer than they are but most of the time it will distort the view so that only negative things are seen, or only those things that reinforce limiting beliefs.

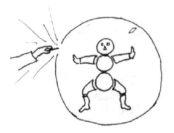

In this story, the first doctor would want a lot of time to work out how to remove the bubble. They will need to look at it from many different angles, and to understand the potential consequences of removing it. The second doctor would know that the bubble can be burst without any ill effects. The person will then be able to see reality clearly, good and bad.

Note that for a story to represent the casting aside of script messages, we need something that does not belong. The monkey, parrot and bubble are obviously not naturally attached to people. If the visual story were based on special spectacles, or even a hood, it would not be as effective because people do really wear these.

It is also important to word the stories so that the grown-ups are providing these imaginary objects to be helpful and protective. However unskilled and misguided parents are, they do the best they can. We can help people feel free of their limitations without any need to blame someone for what happened in the past.

SECTION 5: FRAMES OF REFERENCE

IOKYOK OR SHNOK

One way to introduce the concept of life positions is to ask:

Are you an IOKYOK or a SHNOK?

This idea comes from John Wilson (1975) and is a gimmicky way of saying:
I'm OK, You're OK or Somebody Here's Not OK!

WINDOWS ON THE WORLD

Using the term *OK Corral* (Ernst 1971) for life positions is not always helpful. Some people are not familiar with cowboy films. It reminds others of the American origins of TA and they sometimes assume that TA is therefore not relevant outside the USA. I prefer to use *Windows on the World* as this does not fix the idea geographically or historically. Figure 5.1 shows an illustration for this.

Figure 5.1: Windows on the World

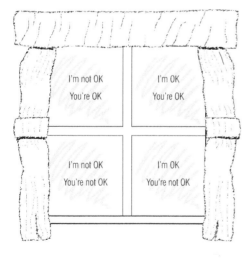

Whether you refer to the OK Corral or to Windows, it helps if the not-OK life positions are taught as 'normal' and not described as pathological.

The Open Window

I often feel that the four life positions described by Berne are not of the same logical level. Thus, when I teach the concept, I find myself explaining that *I'm OK, You're OK* is a reality whereas the other three positions are perceptions. I have also found that people within some religious groups believe firmly that the reality is *I'm not OK, You're not OK*; Okness for them is reserved for their God.

Several years ago, I recall a colleague, Corinne Gledhill, presenting her idea that *I'm OK, You're OK* can also be negative, when it leads someone to trust others inappropriately.

I suggest, therefore, that we take the basic stance as *I am, You are, or just I, You*. We could then have all four existing positions as unhelpful perceptions. We could treat the familiar 2 x 2 diagram as about unhelpful perceptions, as shown in Figure 5.2.

Donkey Bridge Variations

Alliteration for this gives three sets of donkey bridges for this version as shown in Figure 5.3.

Whichever version we use, for assertiveness training it is worth noting that we now have three or four rather than the usual two non-assertive ways of behaving. The third, based on *I'm not OK, You're not OK*, is particularly relevant when we focus on dealing assertively with others. This apathetic, often cynical style is often harder to cope with than someone being aggressive or over-adapted. Optionally, there is also the 4th which is rather like an *I'm Nice, You're Nice* position - and hence too 'nice' to get anything resolved.

Figure 5.2: An Open Window to Reality

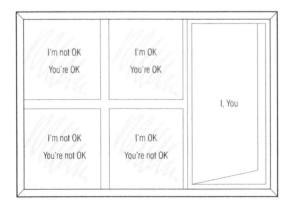

Figure 5.3: Window Variations

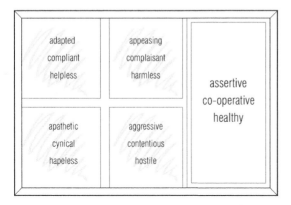

More Windows

Tony White (1994) raised doubts about the life positions when he challenged us to admit that in the more developed countries we actually operate an *I'm **very** OK, You're* OK type of view (which he showed as I ++, You +). He also suggested we use a question mark instead of a plus or minus sign, to indicate that for some people (narcissists) the other person is so unimportant that they don't even rate in terms of OKness. Hence + = OK, - = not OK and ? = irrelevant. This gives us some more 'windows' to look through, as shown in Figure 5.4. I have found that this is often particularly enlightening to people who are new to TA, although those already familiar with with the original version sometimes shift into one of the unhelpful positions when shown something different.

Figure 5.4: More Windows

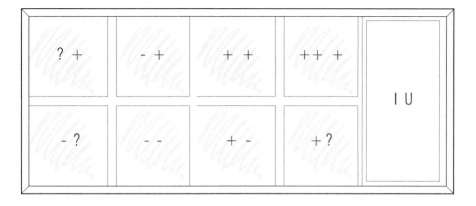

DISPOSITION DIAMOND

This is based on the *Drama Diamond* suggested by Graham Barnes (1981). It makes the point that life positions can be applied to our behaviour and feelings as well as our attitudes. Using a diamond gives a visual representation of the fact that we see behaviour most, but that there are sharp points to our attitudes and feelings.

Often there will be a different life position in effect at each level. I'm not OK, You're OK attitudes, for example, may show up as I'm OK, You're not OK behaviour and mask a feeling of I'm not OK, You're not OK.

In Barnes' material and in my own previous writing, only the original three not-OK positions have been referred to. Perhaps we should now imagine this diamond as three dimensional with some vertical divisions that mean we present different facets at different times. In this way, we might have varying combinations of the range of options shown in Figure 5.5.

Figure 5.5: Disposition Diamond

SECTION 6:   STYLES AND STATES

PERSONAL STYLES

Personal styles is the label I use for behavioural ego states - i.e. the diagnoses we make if we use only observable behaviour as a source of data. I use the three stacked circles as a diagram for this because it is so well known, and I show both positive and negative characteristics for each style.

I refer to Functional Adult within this model, to distinguish it from Adult as described by Berne. Functional Adult refers to behaviour only, so the person is not necessarily in the here-and-now. This avoids the confusion caused by mixing up Berne's Integrated Adult, with its thoughts, feelings and behaviours, with descriptions of logical behaviour only. This also captures the logical, rational and potentially task-focused nature of the behaviour, which can of course be negative when exhibited in inappropriate circumstances.

Figure 6.1: Personal Styles (Behavioural Ego States)

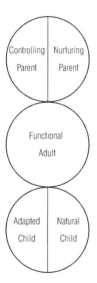

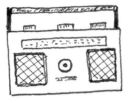

Wavelengths

When introducing ego states, the everyday image of a radio is helpful. We are all like radios, emitting signals across a variety of wavelengths. The wavelengths correspond to behavioural ego states; if we choose very different radio stations we may not like each other (e.g. a pop music type and a classical music type may not get on).

Some people fail to tune in clearly to a wavelength, so their communication is garbled. Some switch wavelengths so fast we can't track them. Others are stuck in the same wavelength all the time - their tuning knob has rusted into place. Some people are not even turned on!

Internal Ego States

When they learn about ego states and transactions, most people soon realise that their outward behaviour does not always correspond to the way they feel inside. I therefore use a separate model for internal ego states, drawn with dotted lines to make the point that these cannot be observed (just as Berne used for ulterior transactions).

I extend these to explain structural ego states and rubberbanding (another great image of what happens to us).

Figure 6.2: Internal Ego States

Figure 6.3: Internal Parent

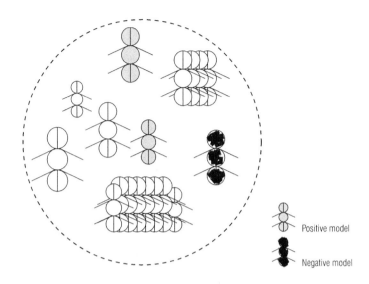

Positive model

Negative model

Thus, Internal Parent contains copies of parent figures in various combinations as shown in Figure 6.3; we pick up on their observable behaviour from their outward ego states and I add little arms and legs to these for effect within the diagram. Everyone we have ever known is captured there in some way.

Long-term caregivers may have provided many copies which may be shown as a series, or as a large entry if there is little variation. They may crowd out other options. Significant others may have resulted in few entries but with extra intensity.

We can add arms and legs to this circle and show that Internal Parent can feel as if we are full of bees. Sometimes the bees are industrious worker bees, and when threatened they may buzz around in a fairly alarming or confusing manner.

Internal Child consists of recordings of ourselves. This can be likened to the rings of a tree, as shown in Figure 6.4. The outer ring is the present, which at this very moment is being formed into another ring.

There are trees in Australia that stop growing during the years of drought. Unfortunately people are not able to do this so our rings may well include some that are not as healthy as they might be. There are likely also to be knots in the tree, representing trauma. However, most of us will also have some healthy rings, plus areas where things went really well for us.

Figure 6.4: Internal Child

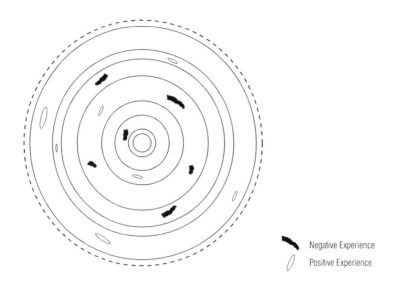

Negative Experience

Positive Experience

Figue 6.5 shows an illustration of our Internal Adult as if it might be the processing part of a computer. It works extremely fast, enabling us to take in data from the outside

Figure 6.5: Internal Adult

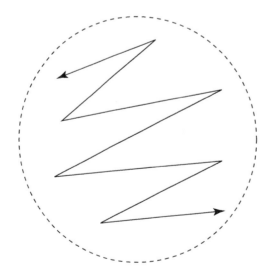

world, access our Internal Child to check that our emotional response is a current one and not a rubberband, access our Internal Parent for ideas on how we might now respond, make a decision, and send an appropriate signal to the behavioural ego state(s) we choose to use.

DECISION MAKING

We can incorporate ego states into a decision making process (NOICISED is DECISION spelled backwards) as follows:

Need	Why do I need to make a decision?
	Why now?
Objective	What do I want to achieve:
	in the short term?
	in the long term?
Information	What information do I have:
	about the problem?
	about possible decisions?
	What information do I still lack?
	How can I get it?
Strategies	How can I achieve what I want?
	How else?
	And how else?
	Are these the only options?
Investigate	What is good about each option?
	What are the snags with each option?
	How might I get round the snags?
Choose	Which option is most likely to help me meet my objective?
	Are there clear second and third choices?
Ego States:	
Internal Parent	What does my previous experience tell me about each option?
Internal Child	How do I feel about each option?
Internal Adult	What is the probability of success with each option?
Decide	Which action am I most likely to be successful with?
	What action(s) will I take to ensure I reach my objective?

THINKING STYLES

We can use the diagram for internal ego states to represent our thinking styles, as shown in Figure 6.6. IP contains our store of experience, IC our emotions and IA conducts evaluation, in response to an event that occurs within our current environment.

Creativity

Creativity can also be illustrated using the internal ego states diagram as shown in Figure 6.7

Figure 6.6: Thinking Styles

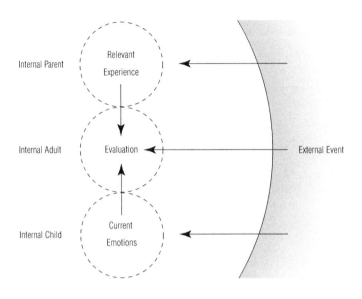

WORKING STYLES

Working styles is my alternative label for *drivers* (Kahler 1975). Drivers are counterscript; they are the ways the grown-ups encourage us to behave so that we will fit their expectations of 'good' behaviour. Much of this behaviour therefore appears to be a strength. The key phrase then becomes:

Too much of a good thing!

Introducing drivers in this way makes it easier for people to admit to having them, and hence increases their chances of bringing these compulsive (driven) behaviours under conscious control.

The names of the drivers are donkey bridges already: **Hurry Up**, **Be Perfect**, **Try Hard**, **Be Strong** - and I use **Please People** for the fifth. This means that the same terms can be used for all five drivers/working styles whether they come from Child or Parent (instead of needing to use Please People, Please Me).

To make them even more memorable, we can act them out as we describe them - talking very fast for Hurry Up, very carefully and with long words for Be Perfect, with a struggle for Try Hard, monotonously for Be Strong, and with a questioning, anxious demeanour for Please People.

Figure 6.7: Creativity and Ego States

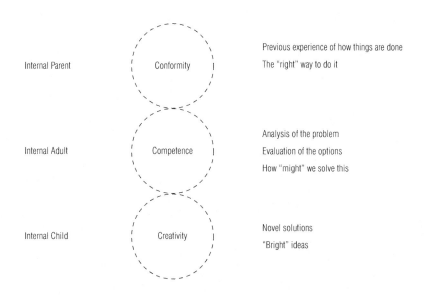

Internal Parent — Conformity — Previous experience of how things are done / The "right" way to do it

Internal Adult — Competence — Analysis of the problem / Evaluation of the options / How "might" we solve this

Internal Child — Creativity — Novel solutions / "Bright" ideas

Another option is to produce pen pictures - short descriptions of how someone with an extreme working style might appear. These can be related to any kind of work, or personal activities, and should include some of the strengths plus an indication of what happens when the strengths are overdone. Use unisex names if possible to avoid people drawing conclusions about gender stereotypes: otherwise think about avoiding a female name for Please People and a male for Be Strong as these are the most obvious stereotypes. Remember also to choose names from different cultures where appropriate.

SECTION 7: STROKES

We can create donkey bridges for stroke preferences related to working styles (see AP[3] in Section 9) do they prefer to be stroked as a person, for their performance, as politeness requires only, for play or for their productivity.

When we remind people to stroke the behaviour they want others to exhibit, it is also important to go back to Berne's definition of positive and negative strokes. Berne linked positive and negative to life positions. Positive strokes invite I'm OK, You're OK. Negative strokes invite one of the other, not OK, positions. This means that constructive criticism is a positive stroke; destructive criticism is a negative stroke. So when we do as suggested in *The One Minute Manager* (Blanchard & Johnson 2004) and "catch them doing something right", it is still sensible at times to tell them how they can improve on what they are doing.

GIVING AND GETTING

When people look at their stroking patterns, they can make notes about what they **give** and what they **get**. For instance, have them identify 5 people they work closely with and sketch out the pattern – positive or negative strokes, how intense (low, medium, high), what about, how often, etc. Then they review the patterns coming in and going out, as well as checking for **swapsies** - those interactions that seem to cancel each other out such as when a compliment is responded to instantly with a return compliment - for example: "Your hair looks good." gets back "Your blouse is pretty."

MOTIVATION LOCATION

A novel way of involving people in exploring their stroking patterns is to combine TA and NLP (neuro-linguistic programming) and invite them to consider where they locate their strokes. Within NLP there is a pre-supposition (among others) that we have specific locations in which we store our beliefs. If we think about what we believe, we can become aware of imaginary physical positions for different beliefs. (Try it - it really does work.) Our location filing system is quite specific, so that we generally have separate locations for beliefs that we hold strongly, beliefs that we are not sure about, and beliefs relating to things other people believe but which we disbelieve.

Our stroke pattern is an analysis of the ways in which we tend to give and receive strokes. There will usually be strokes that we accept and strokes that we reject. It's as if we let some strokes in but keep others out. We may even tell the person that we are rejecting the stroke, as when we say someone else deserves the credit or the blame, or that we were just doing our job. We will of course still remember the strokes that were offered. It is as if we have a separate place outside ourselves where we can keep the strokes without feeling the impact within us.

Using the idea of locations, we can identify where we store our strokes. For example, we probably have different places for positives and negatives, for strokes about appearance versus strokes about performance, for strokes we 'earn' and those given to us unconditionally. We can explore our own patterns in terms of the territory it occupies for us. Having explored, we can decide to accept positive strokes that we previously rejected and to reject negative strokes that we previously accepted.

To accept more positive strokes:
1. identify the location of positive strokes you have been accepting in the past. This will be location A - Accepted.
2. identify a location for strokes you receive that you have doubts about - strokes that you believe may or may not be true. This is location D - Doubtful.
3. identify where you have been putting the positive strokes that you have been rejecting and now want to accept. Label this R - Rejected.
4. move strokes around as follows:
   a. shift A to the location for D and back again (for practice).
   b. shift R to the location for D for a moment
   c. and then move it on to the location for A and allow it to stabilise.

You may need to add more detail to stabilise the new sensation of being stroked. Check and adjust as you imagine receiving and accepting the desired strokes in future.

Then continue to enjoy the sensation as real people give you the same strokes in future. Repeat the process for strokes that you give out if you want to have even more of a positive impact in your interactions with other people.

Figure 7.1: Motivation Location

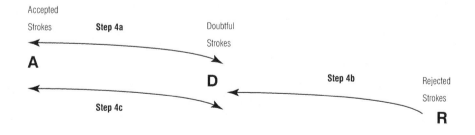

WARM FUZZY TALE

The story associated with strokes is probably the best known one in TA - the Warm Fuzzy Tale by Claude Steiner (1969). Although the content of this is now dated, the moral is still very clear. If we keep giving out positive strokes then so will everyone else.

I amend the tale to change the 'Hip Woman' in Steiner's version into an identity that could be referring to me as the trainer who is teaching TA to people. I also change the reference to warm fuzzies being like a little girl's hand - little boys' hands are just as special.

My amended version, with grateful acknowledgements to Steiner for the original idea, is as follows:

Once upon a time there was a land where everyone was very happy. Each person was born with a magic bag which contained an endless supply of warm fuzzies. When these were handed out to other people, they were like the touch of a small child's hand - so that people felt warmth and caring whenever they received a fuzzy. And because the bags were magic, everyone could ask for and get as many warm fuzzies as they wanted.

One day a wicked witch arrived and started a rumour that there would not always be enough fuzzies in the bags. (The witch wanted to sell potions that bring happiness so the free fuzzy supplies were very bad for business.) People started to hold their fuzzies back in case the rumour was true, so just as in the financial markets they ended up causing it to become true.

Now the land was not so happy. People gave out fuzzies only sparingly, and even then they wanted one in return each time. Someone invented cold pricklies, which stimulated unpleasant feelings but at least reminded people that they were alive. The wicked witch made a lot of money selling misery cures.

A group of people got together and invented plastic fuzzies, where it felt for a moment as if a warm fuzzy had been received but then it became apparent that there was no real feeling behind it from the giver.

Eventually a wise traveller came along, saw what had happened and told people that the bags WERE magic and that the more warm fuzzies they gave out, the more would be generated. Some people started to believe the traveller and began to give out more fuzzies. We are now waiting to see them succeed in changing the fuzzy-giving pattern for the better.

The Warm Fuzzy Tale encourages people to make a start at changing their own stroking patterns without waiting for everyone else to change first. It sends the message that you can generate positive strokes by giving them. It is particularly helpful when told within organisations that are making culture changes and want to foster a healthier psychological working environment.

SOLUTION STROKING

Solution stroking is a technique for encouraging innovation and problem solving. Whenever someone offers you a solution to a problem, resist the temptation to tell them why their idea will not work. Instead, solution stroke by:

1. paraphrasing their idea to demonstrate that you have heard it (and to check that you have understood it!)

2. offering at least one comment (perhaps 2 or 3) about why it is a useful idea (you may have to think hard about it to do this - this will be good for you!)

3. using a question to point out a snag (e.g. "Do you have an idea for raising the funds?" rather than "It would cost too much.")

These steps serve as three powerful strokes. You have therefore reinforced the behaviour of offering solutions. This is much more effective than raising objections to the idea. With solution stroking, they will continue to come to you, bringing fresh ideas - and some of these may be just what you need.

SECTION 8:   **TRANSACTIONS**

INSIDE AND OUTSIDE

The internal ego states described in Section 6: Styles and States can be combined with the diagram of behavioural ego states, or personal styles, as shown in Figure 8.1. This takes care of the differences in 'diagnosis' between people who notice only behaviour and people who intuit 'where someone is coming from'.

This presentation is much simpler than working with the structural and functional ego state models, and takes into account that on a day-to-day basis people are not able to check the historical and phenomenological diagnoses that are required, alongside behavioural and social, to get a complete diagnosis of the ego state that is functioning at any particular time. It is not a good idea to ask an angry customer if their father used to behave like that, or if they realise they have regressed into a childhood tantrum!

Figure 8.1: Inside and Outside

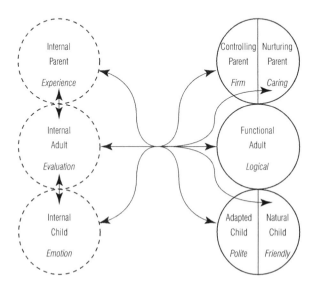

REFRACTED TRANSACTIONS

If we use just the behavioural ego states model, we have a simple way to explain what happens when someone reacts to a different ego state to the one being presented.

Figure 8.2 shows this applied to a conversation between a manager and a new employee. The manager uses Controlling Parent to 'tell' the employee's Adapted Child what to do. However, the employee is young and keen and unused to the parent-child dynamics of organisational life, so responds with a Functional Adult question aimed at the manager's Functional Adult. Because the manager has such a fixed frame of reference, this Functional Adult interaction gets 'refracted'. In the same way that objects under water appear to be in a different place to their real position, the interaction 'appears' to the manager to come from Adapted Child.

To the manager, this is doubly unacceptable: the response should have been Adapted Child polite and instant obedience to the order given; and children are not supposed to question their elders. Hence, the manager becomes even more insistent from Controlling Parent – and the new employee realises that it is better to just follow orders and not bother to do any thinking.

Figure 8.2: A Refracted Transaction

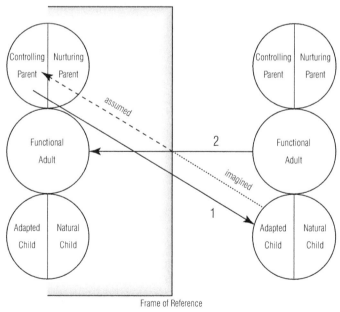

Frame of Reference

1 - Do this right away!

2 - Why do we do it like that?

ULTERIOR TRANSACTIONS

To stay consistent, we need to show inside and outside for ulterior transactions, as shown in Figure 8.3. This also helps explain how we may need to address both the overt behaviour and the unspoken (and possibly out of awareness) message.

Figure 8.3: An Ulterior Transaction

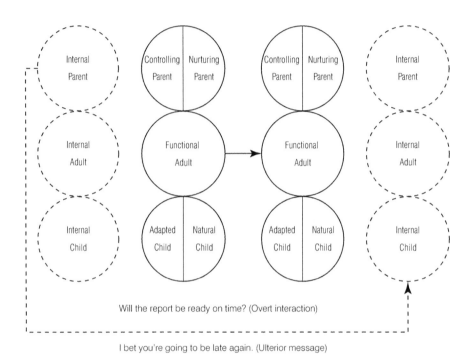

Will the report be ready on time? (Overt interaction)

I bet you're going to be late again. (Ulterior message)

Figures 8.4 shows how this applies to complaint handling. For this, we need an unbroken sequence of interactions that address in turn the angry behaviour of Controlling Parent, the scared Internal Child and the Internal (here-and-now) Adult via the behavioural Functional Adult.

Figure 8.5 shows what happens during conflict. The angry Controlling Parent behaviour is hiding a scared Internal Child. The problem is that the angry Controlling Parent stimulates scared Internal Child in the other person as well, so they also shift to behaving as a Controlling Parent. Person No. 1 then feels even more threatened in Internal Child so calls up (unwittingly) their copies of a grandparent or some similar figure who was more powerful than their parents. Person No. 2 responds in kind, so the conflict becomes an acting out by increasingly powerful forbears.

Figure 8.4: Stages of Conflict

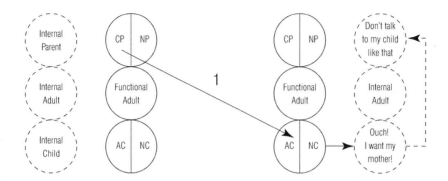

1 - Change this report

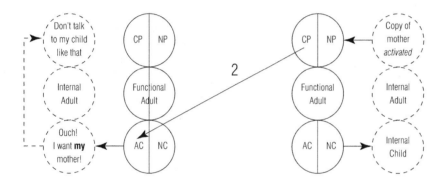

2 - No. It's correct as it is.

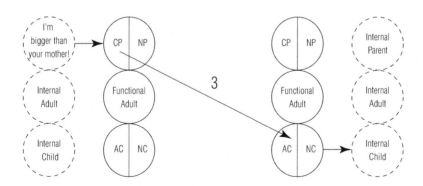

3 - I insist that you change it

Figure 8.5: A Complaint Handling Sequence

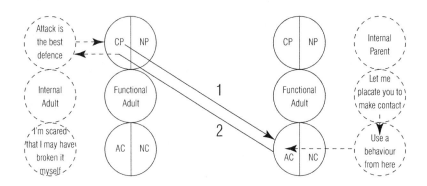

1 - I demand a refund.
2 - I'm sorry you're not satisfied. Sir/Madam.

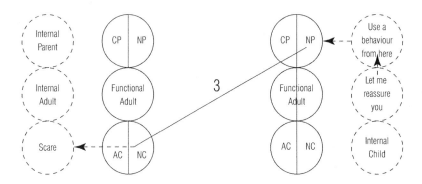

3 - I'm sure we can sort this out.

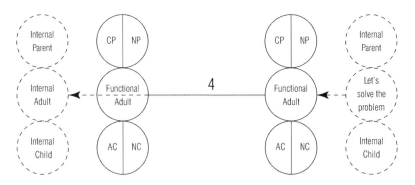

4 - Where is the broken part?

SECTION 9: AP³ – THE ASSESSING CUBE

This is based on Taibi Kahler's (1979) *assessing quadrant*, with one dimension renamed (involving-withdrawing becomes people-alone), and an additional dimension added so that it becomes three dimensional. I also simplify it so that it is easier for people to remember. It can be linked with transactions, strokes and drivers.

Warning - the more that it is simplified and added to, the less it relates to 'real' people, who are always far more complicated than any model. With that caveat in mind, it can still be a useful framework to help people recognise, respect and respond to differences.

Using the first two dimensions we get the four basic 'types'; to add the third dimension on two-dimensional paper is not easy but it is shown with a dotted line in the diagram. Note that it is not at right angles to the other axes but travels from top back right to bottom front

Figure 9.1: AP³ Basic Dimensions

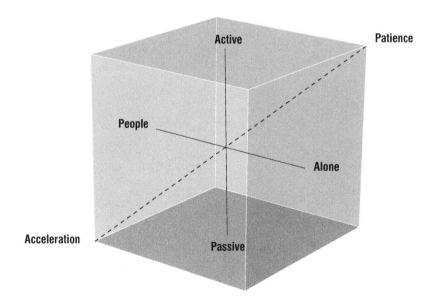

left. This is because the model is based on empirical findings and people do not vary in accordance with an 'ideal' three-dimensional model!

The third dimension allows us to add a fifth type that is based on the Hurry Up working style - hence Acceleration.

The dimensions are:
- **active-passive** - do we move toward others and/or goals or wait for them to move toward or be imposed on us
- **alone-people** - do we prefer to be alone or with a group of people
- **acceleration-patience** - do we do things quickly or do we take our time

THE AP³ SEQUENCE
We also introduce a sequence of likely sources of evidence as we meet people, as shown in Figure 9.2. Paying attention to each of these in turn can help us choose the most effective mode to interact with each person.

THE ABC OF AP³
We can use AP³ to show 'clusters' of what you are likely to notice for each box, as shown in Figure 9.3. Identifying the sector that an employee most occupies gives valuable clues about how they are most likely to want to be managed.

Figure 9.2: The AP³ Sequence

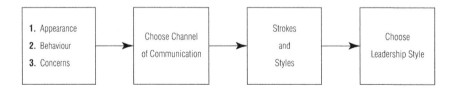

Figure 9.3: The ABC of AP³

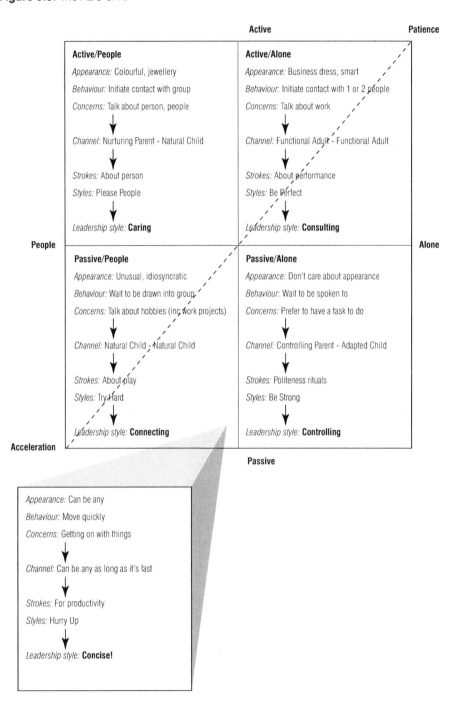

SECTION 10: **INTERNAL PROCESSES**

RRR (said like a growl or as the 3 R's of Feelings)

The Haimowitz's (1976) talk about feelings being of 3 types:
- **racket feelings** - those customary feelings we have that appear to make other people do what we want (like gangster's rackets) e.g. as soon as we look only a little angry, people back away rather than risk becoming the target when we lose our temper
- **rubberbands** - feelings that are replays of the past e.g. someone speaks in a way that reminds us of a teacher and we feel just as we did at 8 years old
- **reactions** - emotions that are related to our current circumstances, in the here-and-now

Note that I do not refer to reactions as genuine feelings. This is because racket feelings and rubberbands feel genuine to the person while they are experiencing them, and they may still feel the same afterwards - we are not always able to recognise when we lose touch with the present.

BBB

BBB – body, breathing, brain - is a useful way to let people know that they have control over their emotions. Have them role-play emotions (mimed to limit the impact) and you can demonstrate how these can be changed via:
- **body** – change posture
- **breathing** – change speed or depth
- **brain** – check rationality of thinking

BAR

I convert the racket system from Erskine and Zalcman (1979), that shows how people get locked into self-fulfilling prophecies, into a diagram that looks like the bars of a prison, with each step named so as to spell BAR.

Beliefs include:
- **core beliefs** - such as our life positions or windows on the world
- **operational beliefs** - such as "I'm shy" or "Nobody cares about me"

Figure 10.1: BARs to Success

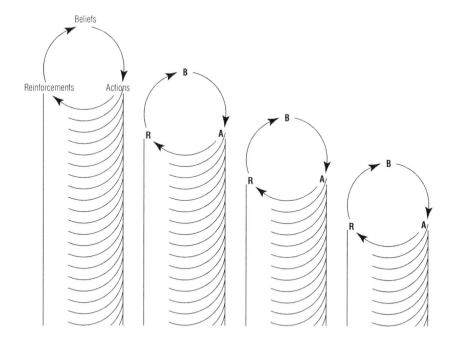

Actions include:

- **observable behaviour** - what do people see us do
- **body sensations**, such as sweating, tension in shoulders, butterflies in stomach
- **fantasies** - imagining the worst

Reinforcements include:

- **reactions** of others - how they behave
- **reinforcing memories** - we recall all the other unpleasant occasions
- **evaluation** of our fantasies - and we may decide that it is even worse than we imagined!

We can break the BARs wherever we think the weakest point is. For some that will be at beliefs; learning about TA models often helps here. Or it may be at the action stage - if we act as if we are confident even though we don't believe it, most people will respond to the confidence. Or perhaps we work on the reinforcement stage by joining a support group, where other participants respond to us as if we are behaving confidently even when we are not.

Figure 10.2: PRO Success

PRO

We can also substitute a positive cycle, PRO, as shown in Figure 10.2. In this, the labels become Positive Beliefs, Resourceful Actions and Okay Outcomes.

ESCAPE

Mary Tobin suggested an alternative to PRO, using the word ESCAPE to stand for Existing Situation, Considered (or maybe Constructive) Action, and Positive Enforcement.

STEPS TO SUCCESS

Another TA concept that helps us understand why people sometimes seem determined to keep their problems is *discounting*. The treatment levels in the *Discount Matrix* (Mellor

---

Figure 10.3: Steps to Success

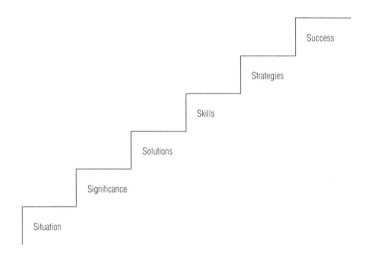

& Schiff 1975) can be converted into a set of steps as shown in Figure 10.3. If we aim to help someone, we must remember to start at the step they are on. If we start further up the steps than they are, they will not understand our comments. The steps are:

Step 1 – Situation   what is happening?

Step 2 – Significance   how is it a problem?

Step 3 – Solutions   what might be done?

Step 4 – Skills   can they make the necessary change, or how can they acquire the skills to do so?

Step 5 – Strategies   how will they implement the change?

Step 6 – Success   do they have the necessary commitment?

We can recognise these steps within organisations as six patterns:

Pattern 1   we discount the stimulus; we fail to notice what is happening

Pattern 2   we are aware of the evidence but do not recognise its significance; we do not realise that it reflects an underlying problem

Pattern 3   we recognise there is a problem but do not believe that anything could be different; we do not believe that anything can be changed

Pattern 4   we accept that things could be different but do not believe that the people involved in our situation could behave any differently; we do nothing because we doubt that anyone has the skills or abilities to change

Pattern 5   we do not believe that we or others are capable of implementing a solution; we decide that the idea is unworkable or will not really resolve the current problem

Pattern 6   we plan implementation but have little real commitment to change; we make no effort to inspire those around us; we take people for granted

Using our knowledge of the patterns as treatment levels, we can design structured processes and introduce confrontation and support so that individuals within organisations can learn to identify and deal with discounting. As shown in Figure 10.4, we can:

1. start from the step they are standing on
2. hold their hand (metaphorically)
3. and lead them up at their own pace.

Figure 10.4: Helping them up the Steps

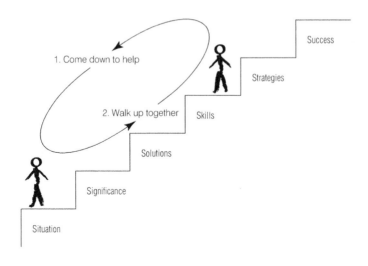

Even if they are higher up the steps, it can be helpful to start back at Situation to ensure they are working on the right problem.

SECTION 11: **BEHAVIOUR PATTERNS**

TIME STRUCTURING

Time structuring can be linked to strokes to show how we build up relationships by exchanging strokes at increasing levels of intensity, as shown in Figure 11.1.

For this, I adjust Berne's descriptions to have *withdrawal* as the only time structure that involves being alone. I often refer to it as *alone* to make it clearer that this generates no direct strokes from others. I use the extra category of *play* as suggested by Cowles-Boyd &

Figure 11.1: Time Structuring and Strokes

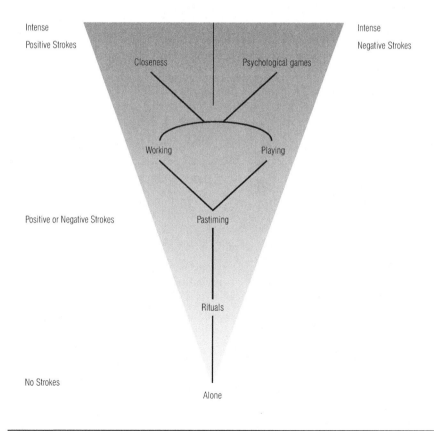

Intense
Positive Strokes

Intense
Negative Strokes

Closeness

Psychological games

Working

Playing

Positive or Negative Strokes

Pastiming

Rituals

No Strokes

Alone

Boyd (1980), so that activity becomes *work* and *play*. Finally, I call *intimacy closeness* as this avoids misunderstandings about sexual intimacy. With an appropriate audience, I would point out that each time structure may involve sex (seriously with an audience of therapists, jokingly with an audience of managers).

- At withdrawal, or when we are physically or psychologically alone, we are not exchanging strokes.
- Rituals provide low intensity strokes.
- Pastiming strokes are a bit more intense because we now have to listen to each other more to keep the conversation flowing.
- Work and play strokes are much more intense.
- We may then opt for games or closeness, depending on what we have learned about each other subconsciously as we moved up the stroke intensity scale together.

GAMES

Games provide powerful negative strokes. We all know that negative strokes are better than no strokes at all. Games are failed attempts at closeness (intimacy). Knowing this enables us to maintain the ***silver lining*** (Section 4) key to human behaviour - we assume that the person has good intentions that are buried beneath their behaviour.

The **Velcro** mentioned earlier as a gimmick provides a demonstration of how it takes two to play a psychological game. If we have no hooks, we cannot be hooked into a game.

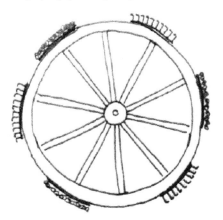

An extended image is to have people imagine they are cartwheels. The rims of the cartwheels are edged with Velcro. As we roll around the world, we come into contact with other cartwheels. If their Velcro coating corresponds to ours, our hooks connect and we engage in a game. If the hooks are different, we may roll right past each other or we may be able to stay in contact without difficulty. Perhaps we can join together under the same cart to shift a bigger load between us than we could do as individuals.

I have renamed some games because the original labels were increasingly perceived as discriminatory. I now call *NIGYSOB* **Gotcha!**, *Rapo* has become **Rebuff**, and *Wooden Leg* is **Millstone** (as in around my neck).

Os Summerton (1992) provided as with a donkey bridge for the roles engaged in a game: **snipers**, **saviours**, **scapegoats**, **stage manager**s, and **spectators**, to which Rosemary Napper (2009) adds **stooges**.

STONES IN THE PITCHER

A story to illustrate the game of **CYG** (Can You Guess – what Berne called *Argentina*):

There was once a teacher who carefully placed large pink rocks into a big open-mouthed pitcher until they were up to the brim, then asked children if the pitcher was full.

When the children said yes, the teacher tumbled in lots of mid-sized shiny green stones, which fell into gaps between the rocks – and asked the children again if the pitcher was full.

When they said yes, the teacher scooped up handfuls of small golden pebbles, which trickled down between the stones and rocks - and asked the children again if the pitcher was full.

When they said yes, the teacher added lots of fine silver sand, which trickled down into the spaces - and asked the children again if the pitcher was full.

When they said yes, the teacher poured in jugs of crystal clear water, which soaked into the sand - and asked the children again if the pitcher was full.

When they said yes, the teacher sprinkled in crunchy white salt, which dissolved into the water - and asked the children again if the pitcher was full.

And the children said no but the teacher had no more to add.

There are several ways this story can be interpreted:

- to show that our perspectives often need to be updated
- to demonstrate how different people will perceive the world differently, often depending on the information they have already (the teacher knew what else was available to put into the pitcher)
- to remind us of how long people tend to cling to perceptions even when it seems obvious to others that they are wrong
- to make the point on time management that you must put in the big rocks first or they will not get done
- and, for a teacher training class, to illustrate an unhelpful psychological game whereby a teacher who knows the answer sets up the class to feel they are stupid.

POTENCY PYRAMID

I have adapted Acey Choy's (1990) *Winners' Triangle* into a **Potency Pyramid**, with corners that match the letters on Karpman's (1968) *Drama Triangle* but turned upside

Figure 11.2: The Potency Pyramid

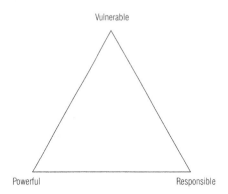

down! Again, the importance of embedded messages within diagrams – flipping it breaks the connection for those who are used to the visual message of the drama triangle diagram.

SECTION 12: **GROUP PROCESSES**

C5P5A5

C5P5A5 is a donkey bridge for understanding and monitoring group processes, developed from an original idea by Landy Gobes (1993). Using PAC catches the attention of people who are familiar with Parent, Adult and Child as the names of ego states. In this case, the PAC stand for:

- **C5** - Context, Contact, Contract, Content, Contrasts
- **P5** – Paradigms, Personal, Professional, Psychological, Parallel
- **A5** - Autonomy, Authentic, Alternatives, Aims, Actions

We could not keep all of these in mind at once but they can be considered roughly chronologically, in the three categories:

- **C5** relates to what is happening as the group starts up.
- **P5** applies once the group has moved into its 'business'.
- **A5** is relevant as the group finishes a task or meeting.

In detail, they are:
- What is the **context**?
- How well are we in **contact**?
- How clear is our **contract**?
- Is the **content** appropriate?
- How are we using our **contrasts**?

- Whose **paradigms** are in effect?
- How are we at the **personal** level?
- How are we at the **professional** level?
- What is happening at the **psychological** level?
- Are there any **parallel** (Searles 1955) processes?

- Are we being **autonomous**?
- Are we being **authentic**?
- Are **alternatives** being generated?
- Whose **aims** are being worked on?
- Are **actions** being committed to?

GROUP IMAGOES

I have renamed Berne's (1966) group imago stages as follows:

Anticipatory   what you have before you come into the group

Adjusted   what you develop as you get to know people – you adjust and/or differentiate the slots

Adapted   how it seems once you've worked out the 'pecking order' or power hierarchy – you've put the slots into positions relative to the leader and decided how and how much to adapt your own behaviour

Attached   what it's like when you have established healthy and close relationships

There may instead be:

Avoidant   when you decide not to proceed to the adjusted imago because you don't want to join the group – you fill the slots with reasons why you don't relate to the people in the group

Alienated   when the group (or you) opts for games instead of attachment

GROUP STAGES – G6

Misel (1975) suggested the stages of a group might be called **Grope**, **Grasp**, **Gripe**, **Group**, and **Groove**. Some would add *Grieve* but that implies that sadness is inevitable whereas the group members may be more focused on moving on to the next (enjoyable) experience so I prefer the more neutral **Go away**.

These can be lined up with the stages above:

Grope as members arrive with **anticipatory** imagoes

Grasp as they begin to get to know who else is in the group and **adjust** their imagoes accordingly, as long as they don't choose **avoidant** instead

Gripe when the group gets gamey and as they sort out how they will **adapt** to each other and who will be in charge – or settle for **alienation**

Group as they start to **attach** to each other

Groove if they really get on well

Go away when it is time to move on top something else

SECTION 13: UNDERSTANDING ORGANISATIONS

BERNE'S DIAGRAMS OF ORGANISATIONS

Berne (1966) drew three diagrams of organisations and called them simple, compound, and complex. He also referred to 'complicated' but did not draw it.

I rename simple as core to get a donkey bridge and produce the diagram of complication by overlaying the complex onto the compound, giving the four diagrams in Figure 13.1. In

Figure 13.1: Berne's Organisational Diagrams

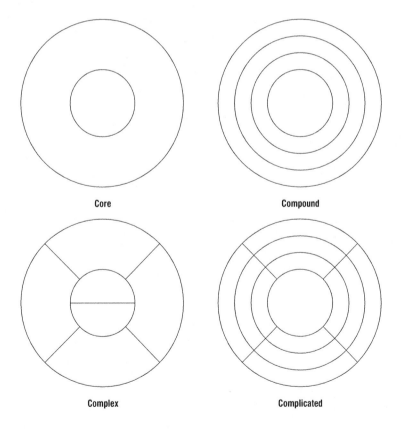

Core   Compound

Complex   Complicated

addition to inviting people to consider which organisational structure might best fit their activities, we can prompt them to consider the pressures that are being exerted across the various internal and external boundaries.

TOP DOWN, BOTTOM UP OR ON THE LEVEL

Organigrams, or organisation charts, tend to be drawn with the senior managers at the top of a pyramid. We can change the impact of the diagram by changing its orientation, as shown in Figure 13.2.

STAGES OF ORGANISATIONS

We can use the ego state model to understand the stages of development of organisations, as shown in Figure 13.3.

In the beginning someone has an idea that needs an organisation for its fulfilment. This may be a new product to be made, a service to offer, a network to set up, or even a new religion. In these early stages the organisation is characterised by **enthusiasm** and **creativity**. People working there are excited, energetic and innovative, and operate mainly from Child ego state. Leadership seems relatively easy, with most interactions being **Natural Child-Natural Child**.

After a while, though, problems arise because no-one is taking care of routine tasks such as getting the bills paid. Duplication starts to become a problem and communication is no longer so easy when the numbers involved have increased.

At this stage, many organisations founder due to lack of adequate organisational procedures. They are troubled by poor cash flow, production problems, erratic quality

Figure 13.2: Top Down, Bottom Up or On the Level

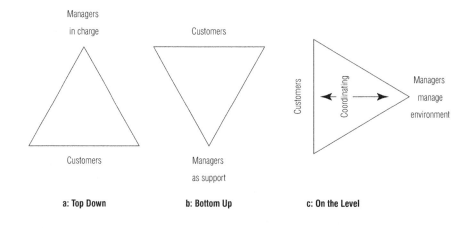

Figure 13.3: Stages of Organisation

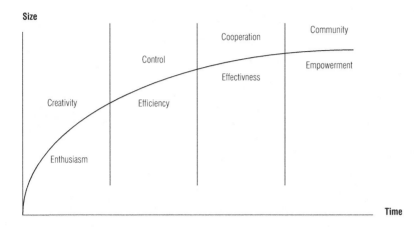

control or similar procedural deficiencies. Those that survive do so by bringing in additional people who make sure that 'proper procedures' are put in place and so add **efficiency** to the enthusiasm that was already there.

These new people are characterised by their use of **control**. They introduce rules and procedure manuals. They often occupy roles as accountants or middle managers and are rewarded by the organisation for taking control. Leadership now tends to focus on **Controlling Parent-Adapted Child** interactions, or **Nurturing Parent-Natural Child** in more paternalistic organisations.

After a time the organisation faces yet another crisis. The 'controllers' become so efficient that they stifle the creativity and enthusiasm of the 'creators'. Innovation ceases, people leave, or spend their time trying to find ways around the system. In a paternalistic culture, they may feel so protected that they come to believe the organisation owes them a living. The organisation is slowly strangled by its own systems.

Organisations which survive the systems crisis do so by bringing in yet another group of people, who focus on getting **co-operation** between the 'controllers' and the 'creators'. These 'co-operators' use mainly Functional Adult ego state, relying neither on Parent experience nor Child emotion. They are Personnel, or Human Resources, or Employee Relations. They aim to help the managers recognise the emotional needs of the staff - and the staff to accept the wisdom and experience of the management.

They bring in training courses in people skills, appraisal schemes, tighter selection procedures, and so on. If these are successful, the organisation continues to grow because they have increased the **effectiveness** with which the efficiency and the enthusiasm are combined. Leadership is now seen to need **Functional Adult - Functional Adult** interactions, with joint problem-solving moving up the agenda.

However, if the organisation remains at this stage, we still have a pattern where some ego states are not in use. We have the equivalent of a *3-person symbiosis*. The bulk of the work force are still mostly in Child, the managers are still operating in Parent, and the Adult is provided by the personnel department.

What is needed is for each individual to recognise that they have all ego states, and to use them. **Empowerment** has become a somewhat hackneyed term but that word captures best the approach that will be needed for the future. The organisation must become a real **community**, where people can utilise their full capabilities.

At this stage the organisation is likely to shrink, because people intuitively sense that true community is difficult to attain with very large numbers. Recession tends to mask the trend towards community because it has meant that organisations have reduced in size considerably in response to market forces. The concept of ego states gives us another explanation for this decrease in organisational size - when we empower people we triple the number of ego states in use!

INNOVATION
We can use the Steps to Success to plan innovation:

Figure 13.4: Steps to Innovation

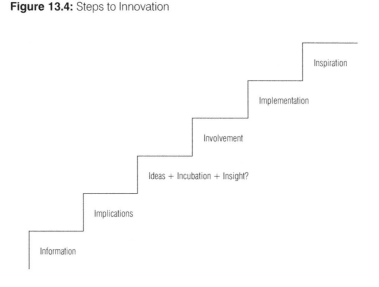

Information	What records do we keep, what statistics are available, how well do we notice what is going on around us?
Implications	What is the significance of whatever we observe? A decrease in sales figures could be a serious problem or could mask the fact that we are actually selling less at higher prices and making more profit. An increase in sales figures could hide a problem if we have put prices too low.
Ideas	We need options and ideas for how things could change. Even impractical ideas are important; truly creative solutions often start from the strangest beginnings.
	There may be two smaller steps within this stage - incubation and insight. **Incubation** occurs when we stop working directly on the problem. Perhaps we sleep on it, or do something else for a while in the hope that we will have a sudden flash of inspiration. **Insight** is when we have that sudden flash of inspiration; when we realise that we know how to solve the problem or at least have the germ of an idea.
Involvement	We need to check out the acceptability and feasibility of our new solution. The views of others will be important, especially if they are affected by the problem or the solution, and even more so if we will be requiring their participation in the implementation.
Implementation	We may have plans to draw up, budgets to obtain, people and resources to organise. We have to work out the practicalities and procedures for putting our ideas into effect.
Inspiration	We need people to be committed to the change. We need to inspire them, particularly when the inevitable snags have to be overcome. There may be unforeseen objections raised by people who were not consulted, or defects in the ideas that become apparent as we put them into effect. If we have moved through the steps, we will be ready to apply the results of our creativity and problem solving.

SAILSHIP SUCCESS

Presenting the organisation as a ship gives a way of illustrating what we must pay attention to if we want to create a culture that will deal effectively with the rapid rate of change. The ship itself can be called **Sailship Success**, the situation becomes the **sea**, problems are **sharks**, we need stability to cope with the waves of change, and the weather represents serendipity (because luck does seem to be a factor in the success or failure of some

Figure 13.5: Sailship Success

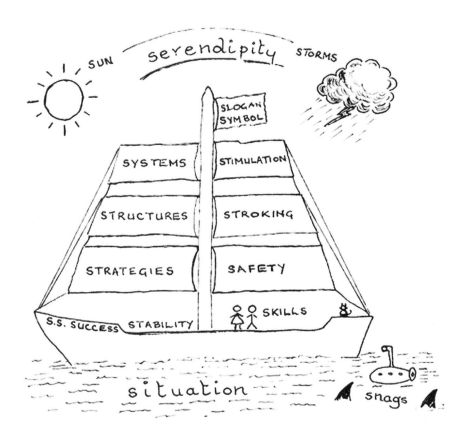

organisations - we cannot always forecast or control events). Serendipity consists of **sunshine** and **storms**.

At a more serious level, the sails provide a reminder of the facets to consider when cultural transformation is required; we can group them into three that are the 'hardware' and three that are the 'software'.

Hardware sails

Strategies   how will the organisation achieve its objectives and implement its vision?

Structures   are they appropriate to the aims of the organisations?

Systems   are these working effectively, are they geared to the structures and strategies?

Software sails

Safety   is there emotional safety: do employees feel able to be open about their concerns; do they trust the organisation to be honest with them? Emotional safety does not imply job security but it does encompass an atmosphere in which such matters are openly discussed.

Stroking   an analysis of the stroking patterns within an organisation will show what needs to change to reinforce the new culture rather than behaviours from the past.

Stimulation   in what ways is creativity fostered and initiative encouraged? What arrangements are made for ongoing development of people? And most important of all, what celebrations are there - events, activities, rituals that reinforce both small and large successes - including initiatives that turn out to be mistakes and which are celebrated as learning opportunities!

Standing on the deck are the people within the organisation, with their range of **skills**, **strengths** and **shortcomings**.

Flying from the mast is the flag, which contains a slogan and possibly a symbol. **Slogans** are an important part of mission statements as they capture the principle in a way that is a constant reminder. **Symbols** have a powerful impact, seeming to 'speak' metaphorically to the mind in a way that words cannot match.

You can also play with this metaphor, inviting people to consider things like who is the **skipper**, or ship's captain, what are the **ship's biscuits** like, what clogs the **sluices**, and so on.

SECTION 14: **LEADERSHIP**

KARMA

For managers who are concerned about the performance of an employee, the following prompts may be helpful *before* looking for psychological reasons:

Knowledge: does the employee know what you want them to do; have you clarified your requirements?

Ability: do they have the ability to do what you want - for example, the intellect, the experience, the physical capability?

Resources: do they have the resources to do what you want - for example, the time, the equipment, the authority over others who are involved?

Motivation: are they motivated to do what you want; are the rewards appropriate; are you sure there are no negative consequences (such as extra work, unpopularity with colleagues, a clash with their own ethics or values)?

Assistance: if the answers to the above four are all yes, then you need to assist the employee in some way - either by providing coaching or training - or by assisting them out of the job!

HIERARCHICAL SYMBIOSIS

Quinten Holdeman (1989) drew a similar diagram to that shown as Figure 14.1, but included Adult within the symbiosis. He also coined the terms Protective Parent or Pillar for the key senior manager in the symbiotic chain and Subordinate Symbiont for the others.

POWER POTENTIALS

A donkey bridge for sources of power:

Physical   e.g. being bigger or smaller
Pecuniary   having control of tangible rewards or penalties
Performance   power by virtue of knowledge, skill or expertise
Personal   shows positively through people skills or negatively through manipulative skills

Figure 14.1: Hierarachical Symbiosis

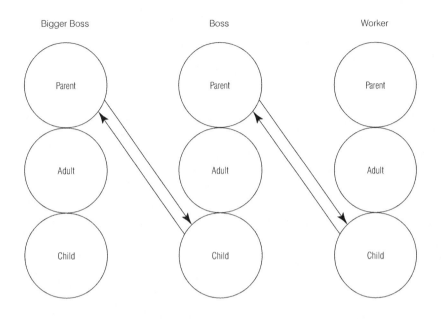

Psychological	positively as charisma, referent power and negatively through ulterior transactions
Positional	comes with the role, the position in the hierarchy, the legal context
Political	based on ideological power, beliefs and values

Note that I do not include 'coercive' because this is behaviour rather than a source of power.

LEADERSHIP STYLES

In Section 9: AP³ – The Assessing Cube we showed leadership styles as they relate to people's preferences. These are shown in Figure 9.2: The ABC of AP³ and are: caring, consulting, controlling, connecting and concise!

The most effective leaders are those who can adopt all of the styles to suit each employee rather than simply leading only from their own style.

SECTION 15:   CHANGE

THE COMPETENCE CURVE

Changes within organisations result in change for individuals. I use Pam Levin's (1982) Cycles of Development to explain the typical process that people experience. I convert it from a spiral into a Competence Curve, showing how our level of competence varies at the different stages.

I point out that these changes are normal, and that a change in an executive, professional, or middle management level job can often take two or more years to complete. Organisations often restructure before the person has a chance to reach the relative comfort of completion!

Figure 15.1: The Competence Curve

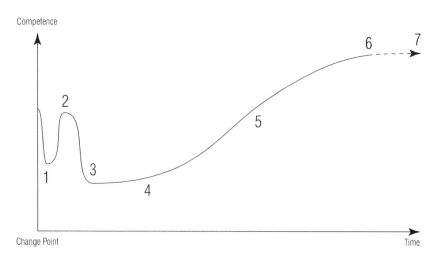

1. Immobilisation
2. Denial
3. Frustration
4. Acceptance
5. Development
6. Application
7. Completion

The Competence Curve is not to scale. Later stages usually take much longer than the early stages, which might be completed in a matter of minutes or hours. They are still significant even though they are relatively short. Also, there will be different time spans for different individuals and for different changes.

1. **Immobilisation** occurs just after the change point and relates to the *Being* stage in Cycles of Development. In the work setting, we need at this stage to feel welcomed without any requirement to perform.

2. **Denial** relates to the *Exploring* (or what Levin called the Doing) stage. We need the time to get used to our new circumstances, explore our environment. We need others to ensure that we can do this within a safe structure.

3. **Frustration** is the equivalent of the *Thinking* stage. We want to think about our new role and what is involved. We need people to be patient and allow us to do our own thinking.

4. **Acceptance** is the *Identity* stage. We now accept that we have gone through a change and will be a different person in some way. We now decide what style of manager, what type of engineer, etc. we are going to be. We need tolerance to make our own choices rather than having a corporate style imposed on us.

5. **Development** is the *Skills/Structure* stage. At last we are ready for training and development within our new role. Many organisations put training far too early, before people have really understood the implications of their new role.

6. **Application** is the *Integration* stage. Now we apply our learning and pull together the previous stages.

7. **Completion** is the *Recycling* stage. We have completed the process of making the change, we no longer feel that we are in the midst of a change, and we are ready for the next change - and for the next stage in our growth.

OBJECTIVE SETTING

Any training course leads to change for the participants. In order to help them move into the Application stage, we can encourage them to set clear, specific objectives for how they will change their behaviour after the course. Three guidelines for 'good' objectives are that they should be:

■ **Measurable** - if we do not state the objective in a way that can be measured, we never get the satisfaction of knowing we have achieved it. 'Give more strokes' is too vague; 'Give three positive strokes a week to Mohammed' allows our **Parent** to check that we are doing our homework - and to reward us.

■ **Manageable** - there is often a temptation after a training course to attempt to change ourselves totally. Instead, we need to tackle manageable amounts. Our **Adult** can work out what is realistic. Giving 50 more strokes a week would be a strain for most people; it is better to aim for 5 and achieve it than 50 and fail.

■ **Motivational** - if our **Child** is not invested in the action plan, we are unlikely to achieve it. We therefore need to check **WIFM** - *what's in it for me?* If we hardly ever see Mohammed, perhaps a better working relationship will not seem that significant to us. However, if Mohammed is our manager, an improvement in our stroking pattern may be very beneficial.

In the UK there are sweets called M&Ms. The sweet manufacturers also make plastic dolls with the letter M on the front. These make a great donkey bridge. I have three medium size figures in different colours that I refer to as Parent, Adult and Child. I also have a larger figure with a movable arm; when pumped it dispenses handfuls of sweets. Even senior managers will queue up for their share when another participant has confirmed that they have written their action plans according to the MMM guidelines.

SPECTRE

We can counteract the tendency to pay attention only to the 'soft' issues (as with Sailship Success) by prompting people to use SPECTRE as a checklist of factors to consider when change is anticipated.

SPECTRE stands for the social, political, economic, competition, technological, regulatory and environmental factors that may affect an organisation (or an individual). For each of these factors, we need to consider what impact they might have – and whether we should be taking action to forestall or encourage such trends.

Social	what are the social factors (e.g. education, family patterns, health, retirement expectations) that affect your organisation; how are cultural norms changing; what about changes in work and home life patterns; how might social developments change the way your organisation is structured or the nature of the people you employ?
Political	what impact do politics have on your organisation; what might happen if the local or national government changes policies or politicians; is your organisation affected by the politics of more than one country; what might happen if political unrest were to occur in any of your spheres of operation; what are the political implications of new areas of business?
Economic	how does the economic climate affect your organisation; what happens when interest rates change; what about international monetary factors; how might changes in sales or purchasing patterns affect your cash flows or other financial aspects; what investments might you need to make?
Competition	what are your competitors working on; what new competitors and/or products might emerge; what impact might competitors have on consumers; how static or volatile are your markets; how are you

marketing your organisation and/or its products; where are you placed in the competitive hierarchy and where do you aspire to be?

Technological   what technological changes are likely to affect your organisation; are you taking maximum advantage of technological advances; what resources might you need to allocate to technology; how might you use new technology to increase organisational effectiveness; how might technology affect your suppliers and your customers?

Regulatory   what legal requirements are likely to affect your organisation and/or your products; how might you have to change your employment practices, your production processes, your marketing strategies; what new regulations might arise which would impact on the ways you and others in your industry or profession behave?

Environmental   what environmental changes might have an impact on your organisation; how might changing requirements for environmental stewardship (e.g. pollution, ethical practices) affect your working processes and/or your costs; what changes might occur to the local environments of your premises; what, if any, of the world's resources are required for your production and are any of these becoming depleted?

SECTION 16: YOUR OWN COMPETENCE

REMEMBERING WHAT TO INCLUDE – D5

Having coached many people in preparation for their final TSTA exams, I have devised the following checklist to apply to each topic you teach:

Definition give the definition you are using, or, for a TA exam, give the definition(s) and the references from the TA literature

Diagram many TA concepts have a diagram. Check for any unintended messages (see my comments earlier about, for example, the impact of the lines entering the child in the script matrix) and, for a TA exam, draw diagrams as the originator did or explain why not

Description explain/describe the concept

Demonstration give an example (or two) of how it can be applied within a professional context

Do with it tell your audience what can be done with the concept, why it is useful, mention any caveats about its application (e.g. likely to stimulate emotional responses)

STAGES OF PRACTICE

There are two optional donkey bridges for stages of professional practices such as counselling, coaching, mentoring etc.

1. **Alliance** – getting to know each other, agreeing what we will be doing together
2. **Assessment** – helping the client to assess their current and potential situations, attributes, skills and knowledge
3. **Analysis** – prompting the client to identify themes and patterns across time and situations
4. **Alternatives** – prompting the client to generate options from which the client will choose
5. **Action planning** – prompting the client to plan what to do, consider contingencies.
6. **Application** – the client implements the action plan, with or without further ongoing support from the practitioner

7. **Auditing** – not really the 7th stage but something that should be continual – this refers to monitoring the relationship as it goes along with a view to constantly enhancing the impact of interactions

In the next set of stages, I 'top and tail' them with two more components, as shown below. The lines are added to make it clearer that there are 5 stages with overarching and underpinning components.

	Supervision	overarching all stages if the practitioner is to be supported and challenged to develop their competence
1.	Starting off	those activities that take place before practitioner and client come together, such as identification of need and finding an appropriate practitioner
2.	Setting up	establishing a clear contract and effective working relationship
3.	Stocktaking	assessing the current situation, skills levels, learning needs, etc of the client
4.	Strategising	working out what needs to be done and doing it, whether this requires 'teaching' from the practitioner or 'practice' by the client
5.	Saying goodbye	ending the relationship in a healthy way instead of letting it 'die' or drift on
	Self awareness	underpinning all stages if the practitioner is to maximise their effectiveness and minimise the impact of their own issues

CONTRACTING FOR SUPER-VISION

Note that using a hyphen in super-vision is a form of donkey bridge. It draws attention to the meaning of the word, in that the intention is to facilitate the supervisee to develop their own super vision, or meta perspective, of their practice.

An easy checklist for the start of each piece of supervision, and that can also be applied as an overall framework, is to think of the three R's – in this case, *results, relationship* and *responsibility*.

Results are what the supervisee wants to achieve in the timeslot - e.g. do they want to clarify their thinking, analyse an intervention, identify options for the future? The supervisor can then check that such a result is realistic in the time available and at the supervisee's level of experience, and that they are competent to supervise such a piece of work.

Relationship refers to how supervisor and supervisee agree to work together for this piece of supervision. Does the supervisee want to be asked questions, allowed to talk, reflected back to, prompted through a structured approach, provided with information, challenged into greater insight, supported with a difficult client, etc?

Responsibility is listed essentially as a reminder that the supervisor is responsible for providing 'good enough' supervision (the best the supervisor can do) and the supervisee is responsible for deciding what to take from the supervision, how to perform in future, what decisions to make when next with the client.

FUNCTIONS OF SUPER-VISION

A helpful way to consider the nature of supervision is through three elements described over 20 years ago by Brigid Proctor (1986). She suggested that supervision includes:

normative the supervisor has a responsibility for ensuring that the practitioner is practising in ways that are competent and ethical; that they are working within whatever professional, organisational and national rules and laws apply; that they are behaving as a good practitioner should.

formative the supervisor has a role in the development and growth of the practitioner; this may be via feedback, direct guidance, role modelling or a variety of other options; the aim is to develop the skills, theoretical knowledge, personal attributes, self awareness, etc, of the practitioner so they become increasingly competent.

supportive the supervisor is there to support the practitioner when the inevitable doubts and insecurities arise; to challenge and confront (supportively!) when the practitioner's personal issues become evident; and to provide a 'safety-valve' when client issues get 'picked up' by the practitioner. (Proctor called this restorative but she was writing about supervision of counsellors, who tend to encounter more 'distressing' client issues than developmental practitioners.)

TRANSFERENCE

When we look more closely at transference, we can identify several formats. Novellino & Moiso (1990), writing of therapy, refer to: the client merging themself with the therapist; the client projecting all of the 'good' or all of the 'bad' that they believe exists within themself onto the therapist; and triadic, where the client projects their own Parent ego state, the content of which has been copied from others, onto the therapist. Clarkson (1991) writes of: complementary, where the client seeks a symbiotic relationship with their therapist; concordant, where the client projects aspects of themself onto the therapist so they seem to be alike; destructive, which is acting out or similar and means therapy cannot proceed; and facilitative transference, where the client chooses a therapist so the client can still use effective behaviour patterns from the past.

Applying these ideas to developmental TA applications, we can categorise on two dimensions:

- projecting elements of our self or of someone else (a third party) onto the person we are transacting with
- projecting so that we appear to get on well with the other person or so that we have a problem relating to each other

Figure 16.1: Transference Formats

Project self

Competitive	Concordant
We project elements of our own Child or Parent ego state onto the other person and then get into a competitive symbiosis about whose Child or Parent will take precedence	We project elements of our own Child or Parent ego state onto the other person and then believe they are just like us and we are empathising with each other
Conflictual	**Co-dependent**
We project elements of 'a third party' onto the other person and then feel we must 'fight' in a Parent-Child or Child-Parent interaction	We project elements of 'a third party' onto the other person and then seek a Parent-Child or Child-Parent symbiosis

Project someone else

Have problem in relating (left axis)

Appear to get on well together (right axis)

Using these two axes provides us with a simplified model of transference with four broad categories, making it easier to think about what is happening between us and our clients or students.

ORIGINAL TA SOURCES

Autonomy - Berne, Eric (1964) *Games People Play* New York: Grove Press

Assessing Quadrant - Kahler, Taibi (1979) *Managing with the Process Communication Model*, Human Development Publications

Cycles of Development - Levin, Pamela (1982) The cycle of development *Transactional Analysis Journal* 12:2, 129-139

Discounting - Mellor, Ken and Schiff, Eric (1975) Discounting *Transactional Analysis Journal* 5:3, 295-302

Drama Diamond - Barnes, Graham (1981) On Saying Hello *Transactional Analysis Journal* 11:1, 22-32

Drama Triangle - Karpman, Stephen(1968) Fairy Tales and Script Drama Analysis *Transactional Analysis Bulletin* 7:26, 39-43

Drivers - Kahler, Taibi (1975) Drivers: The Key to the Process of Scripts *Transactional Analysis Journal* 5:3, 280-284

Game Roles - Summerton, R (1992) The Game Pentagon *Transactional AnalysisJournal* 22:2, 66-75 and Napper, R (2009) Personal communication

Games - Berne, Eric (1964) *Games People Play* New York: Grove Press

Group Imagoes - Berne, Eric (1963) *Structure and Dynamics of Organizations and Groups* Philadelphia: Lippincott

Group Processes - Gobes, Landy (1993) C4P4: A Consultation Checklist *Transactional Analysis Journal* 23:1 42-44

Group Stages - G6 – Misel, Lory (1975) T Stages of Group Treatment *Transactional Analysis Journal* 5:4, 385-391

Hierarchical Symbiosis - Holdeman, Quinten L (1989) The Symbiotic Chain *Transactional Analysis Journal* 19:3, 137-144

Injunctions - Goulding R and Goulding M (1976) Injunctions, Decisions and Redecisions *Transactional Analysis Journal* 6:1, 41-48

IOKYOK/SHNOK - Wilson, John H (1975) IOKYOKs vs the SKNOKs *Transactional Analysis Journal* 5:3, 247-249

Life Positions - Berne, Eric (1962) Classification of Positions *Transactional Analysis Bulletin* 1, 23

OK Corral - Ernst, Franklyn (1971) The OK Corral *Transactional Analysis Journal* 1:4 231-240

Organisational Diagrams - Berne, Eric (1963) *Structure and Dynamics of Organizations and Groups* Philadelphia: Lippincott

Permission, Protection, Potency - Crossman, Pat(1966) Permission and Protection *Transactional Analysis Bulletin* 5(19) 152-154 and Steiner, Clause (1968) TA as a Treatment Philosophy *Transactional Analysis Bulletin* 7:27, 61-64

Physis - Berne, Eric (1957) *A Layman's Guide to Psychiatry and Psychoanalysis* New York: Simon and Schuster (original work published in 1947 as The Mind in Action New York: Simon and Schuster)

Playing (added to Time Structuring) - Cowles-Boyd, L and Boyd H (1980) Play as a Time Structure *Transactional Analysis Journal* 10:1, 5–7

Power - Krausz, R (1968) Power and Leadership *Transactional Analysis Journal* 16:2, 85-94 and Jacobs, A (1987) Autocratic Power *Transactional Analysis Journal* 17(3), 59-71

Racket System – Erskine, Richard and Zackman, Marilyn (1979) The Racket System; a model for racket analysis *Transactional Analysis Journal* 9:1, 51-59

Script - Berne, Eric (1961) *Transactional Analysis in Psychotherapy* New York: Grove Press

Script Matrix - Berne, Eric (1972) *What do you say after you say Hello?* New York: Grove Press

Strokes - Berne, Eric (1964) *Games People Play* New York: Grove Press

Three Cornered Contract - English, Fanita (1975) The Three Cornered Contract *Transactional Analysis Journal* 5:4 383-4

Time Structuring - Berne, Eric (1961) *Transactional Analysis in Psychotherapy* New York: Grove Press

Transference - Novellino, Michele and Moiso, Carlo(1990) The Psychodynamic Approach to Transactional Analysis *Transactional Analysis Journal* 20:3 187-192 and Petruska Clarkson, (1991) *Transactional Analysis Psychotherapy* London: Routledge

Warm Fuzzies -Steiner, Claude A Warm Fuzzy Tale (1969) see http://www.emotional-literacy.com/fuzzy.htm

Winner's Triangle - Choy, Acey (1990) The Winner's Triangle *Transactional Analysis Journal* 20:1, 40-46

WHERE DONKEY BRIDGES
FIRST APPEARED

JULIE HAY

AP[3] - as AP[2] Creating Community - The Task of Leadership *Leadership and Organizational Development Journal* 14 (7) 1993

AP[3] - The Assessing Cube *TA UK* Spring 2001

Autonomy Matrix - *INTAND Newsletter* 5(1) Nov 1997

BARS - *Working it Out at Work* Sherwood Publishing 1993

BBB - *Working it Out at Work* Sherwood Publishing 1993

Behavioural Ego States - *INTAND Newsletter* 2(1) Mar 1994

C5P5A5 - as *C4P5A3 INTAD Newsletter* 1(1) Jan 1993

Coaching Transactions - *INTAND Newsletter* 10(3) Sept 2002

Competence Curve - *Transactional Analysis for Trainers* McGraw Hill 1992

Contracting Levels - as *procedural, professional, psychological, perceptual, political INTAND Newsletter* 8 (4) June 2000

Creativity - *Transactional Analysis for Trainers* McGraw Hill 1992

Decision Making - *Working it Out at Work* Sherwood Publishing 1993

Discounting - the 6 Levels appeared first in *INTAD Newsletter* 1(4) Dec 1993

Disposition Diamond - *Transactional Analysis for Trainers* McGraw Hill 1992

Ego States of the Organisation - *INTAD Newsletter* 1(4) Dec 1993

Hierarchy -P-C only - *Transactional Analysis for Trainers* McGraw Hill 1992

Innovation - *Transactional Analysis for Trainers* McGraw Hill 1992

Internal Ego States and Thinking - *Transactional Analysis for Trainers* McGraw Hill 1992

KARMA - *INTAND Newsletter* 6(2) June 1998

Language Patterns - *INTAND Newsletter* 7(1) Nov 1999

Maybe (story) - *INTAND Newsletter* 8(3) Sept 2000

MMM (Objective Setting) - *INTAD Newsletter* 1(4) Dec 1993

Motivation Location - *INTAND Newsletter* 3(2) June 1995

NOICISED - *Transactional Analysis for Trainers* McGraw Hill 1992

Personal Styles - *Transactional Analysis for Trainers* McGraw Hill 1992

Potency Pyramid - appeared as *Autonomy Triangle* in *Transformational Mentoring* McGraw Hill 1995, Sherwood Publishing 1999

PRO (Success) - *Transactional Analysis for Trainers* 2nd edition Sherwood Publishing 2009

R4C4P4 - Groundrules for Groups - *INTAND Newsletter* 9(2/3) June/Sept 2001

Sailship Success - *INTAND Newsletter* 4(1) Nov 1996

Solution Stroking - *Transactional Analysis for Trainers* McGraw-Hill 1992

SPECTRE - *INTAND Newsletter* 8(3) Sept 2000

Steps to Success - *INTAND Newsletter* 4(3) Sept 1996

Stones in the Pitcher (story) - *INTAND Newsletter* 8(3) Sept 2000Transference - *INTAND Newsletter* 11(1) Nov 2003

Warm Fuzzies (revised) - *INTAND Newsletter* 3(2) June 1995

Windows on the World - with Open Window - *INTAND Newsletter* 8(2) June 2000

Windows on the World - with 8 windows plus open window - Making meaning *IDTA Newsletter* 5 (2) July 2010

OTHER AUTHORS

Group Stages - G6 - Misel, Lory T *Stages of Group Treatment Transactional Analysis Journal* 5 (4) Oct 1975

IOKYOK/SHNOK - Wilson, John H *IOKYOKs vs the SKNOKs Transactional Analysis Journal* 5 (3) July 1975

Game Roles - Summerton, R *The Game Pentagon Transactional Analysis Journal* 22 (2) April 1992 and Napper, R Personal communication 2009

Warm Fuzzies -Steiner, Claude *A Warm Fuzzy Tale* 1969 see http://www.emotional-literacy.com/fuzzy.htm

SHOULDN'T'S Chris Davidson - *INTAND Newsletter* 9(1) Nov 2001

Priest Prophet Pastor - Anne de Graaf - *INTAND Newsletter* 9(2/3) June/Sept 2001

REFERENCES

Allen, Brian (1971) *Suzy and the Parrot Transactional Analysis Journal* 1:3, 36-37

Barnes, Graham (1981) On Saying Hello *Transactional Analysis Journal* 11:1, 22-32

Berne, Eric (1957) *A Layman's Guide to Psychiatry and Psychoanalysis* New York: Simon and Schuster (original work published in 1947 as *The Mind in Action* New York: Simon and Schuster)

Berne, Eric (1961) *Transactional Analysis in Psychotherapy* New York: Grove Press

Berne, Eric (1962) Classification of Positions *Transactional Analysis Bulletin* 1, 23

Berne, Eric (1963) *Structure and Dynamics of Organizations and Groups* Philadelphia: Lippincott

Berne, Eric (1964) *Games People Play* New York: Grove Press

Berne, Eric (1968) (writing as Cyprian St Cyr) The Gordon Knot *Transactional Analysis Bulletin* 7 (23) January

Berne, Eric (1972) *What do you say after you say Hello?* New York: Grove Press

Blanchard K & Johnson S (2004) *The One Minute Manager* New York: HarperCollins

Choy, Acey (1990) The Winner's Triangle *Transactional Analysis Journal* 20:1, 40-46

Cowles-Boyd, L and Boyd H (1980) Play as a Time Structure *Transactional Analysis Journal* 10:1, 5–7

Crossman, Pat (1966) Permission and Protection *Transactional Analysis Bulletin* 5(19) 152-154

English, Fanita (1975) The Three Cornered Contract *Transactional Analysis Journal* 5:4 383-4

Ernst, Franklyn (1971) The OK Corral *Transactional Analysis Journal* 1:4 231-240

Erskine, Richard and Zackman, Marilyn (1979) The Racket System; a model for racket analysis *Transactional Analysis Journal* 9:1, 51-59

Gobes, Landy (1993) C4P4: A Consultation Checklist *Transactional Analysis Journal* 23:1 42-44

Goulding R and Goulding M (1976) Injunctions, Decisions and Redecisions *Transactional Analysis Journal* 6:1, 41-48

Haimowitz, M L & Haimowitz N R (1976) *Suffering is Optional* Haimowoods Press

Hay, J – see list of where donkey bridges first appeared and books by same author listed at front of book

Holdeman, Quinten L (1989) The Symbiotic Chain *Transactional Analysis Journal* 19:3, 137-144

Jacobs, A (1987) Autocratic Power *Transactional Analysis Journal* 17(3), 59-71

Kahler, Taibi (1975) Drivers: The Key to the Process of Scripts *Transactional Analysis Journal* 5:3, 280-284

Kahler, Taibi (1979) *Managing with the Process Communication Model*, Human Development Publications

Karpman, Stephen(1968) Fairy Tales and Script Drama Analysis *Transactional Analysis Bulletin* 7:26, 39-43

Krausz, R (1968) Power and Leadership *Transactional Analysis Journal* 16:2, 85-94

Levin, Pamela (1982) The cycle of development *Transactional Analysis Journal* 12:2, 129-139

Mellor, Ken and Schiff, Eric (1975) Discounting *Transactional Analysis Journal* 5:3, 295-302

Misel, Lory (1975) T Stages of Group Treatment *Transactional Analysis Journal* 5:4, 385-391

Napper, R (2009) Personal communication

Novellino, Michele and Moiso, Carlo(1990) The Psychodynamic Approach to Transactional Analysis *Transactional Analysis Journal* 20:3 187-192 , Petruska Clarkson (1991) *Transactional Analysis Psychotherapy* London: Routledge

Searles H F (1955) *The informational value of the supervisor's emotional experiences* Psychiatry No 18 pp 135-146

Seligman, Martin E. P. (2002) *Authentic Happiness: Using the New Positive Psychology to Realize Your Potential for Lasting Fulfillment.* New York: Free Press

Steiner, Claude (1968) TA as a Treatment Philosophy *Transactional Analysis Bulletin* 7:27, 61-64

Steiner, Claude (1969) A Warm Fuzzy Tale see http://www.emotional-literacy.com/fuzzy.htm

Summerton, R (1992) The Game Pentagon *Transactional Analysis Journal* 22:2, 66-75

Wilson, John H (1975) IOKYOKs vs the SKNOKs *Transactional Analysis Journal* 5:3, 247-249

INDEX